To Dad

Christmas 1983

PELHAM

HORSEMASTER SERIES

Horses and the Law

PELHAM HORSEMASTER SERIES

Horses and the Law

JOHN WEATHERILL

London
PELHAM BOOKS

First published in Great Britain by
PELHAM BOOKS LTD
52 Bedford Square
London WC1B 3EF
1979

ISBN 0 7207 1130 4

Printed in Great Britain by
Hollen Street Press Ltd, Slough, Berkshire
and bound by Redwood Burn, Esher

CONTENTS

INTRODUCTION

One warm, sunny day in early October a young man was walking through a stretch of Norfolk woodland shooting pheasant. He came across a reed-surrounded pond in which a beautiful blonde girl was bathing. His eyes lit up as he approached her and asked, 'Are you game?' She replied 'Yes' – so he shot her; thus illustrating the well-known legal maxim that a slavish adherence to the letter of the law can seriously interfere with the finer things of life. Unfortunately, despite this warning, some knowledge of the law, if not a slavish adherence to its letter, is essential in every walk of life.

Probably the old tag 'ignorance of the law is no excuse' has never been a fair one. If it was unfair in the past, however, how much more so is it today? Since the mid-twentieth century increasingly energetic governments have churned out statutes, orders and regulations, not just by the hundred, but by the thousand, until the stage has been reached where no one can claim to have heard of, let alone understand, even one tenth of them. The result is that the most dutiful citizen daily stands in danger of unwittingly breaking the law.

Of course, in practice, things are not quite as bad as that. What was done legally yesterday is almost certain to be legal today or, if not, the change will have been widely advertised to interested parties. The time of greatest danger comes when embarking on a new venture in which everything, including the law, has to be learnt from first principles and one cannot look back to yesterday's precedent for guidance. Hence the purpose of this book. The following chapters contain an outline to the law relating to most aspects of the ownership and enjoyment of horses in a progressive sequence from the first steps of learning to ride them to the decision to start a business and making a living out of them.

But first a word of warning. It is not intended that this book should be used as a text book – it is too short for that. Rather it is intended as a guide, not to replace proper legal advice, but to indicate where it is necessary and how it may be of help. It will have served its purpose well if it acts as an early-warning device for trouble looming over the horizon and it will have served its purpose even better if it indicates a path towards a trouble-free horizon. Of necessity several aspects of the law have been only sketchily outlined, but where possible references have been given to assist in more detailed study and a list of cases is provided to help trace the references.

At the risk of convincing the reader he is wasting his time in going further, another warning note must be struck. Because of the way the United Kingdom has evolved, the law as stated herein is generally correct only for England and Wales. Up to the Union with Scotland Act 1706 Scottish law developed on a course substantially different from that of England and Wales, and has continued to do so in many important respects. Parliament at Westminster enacts laws equally binding on both sides of the border, but it also enacts laws which apply exclusively to one side or to the other.

Moreover, when not subject to direct rule, Northern Ireland has its own law-making Assembly and the Isle of Man and the Channel Islands also have a substantial measure of legal autonomy. Although an attempt will be made to pin-point these differences it will not always be possible, especially in the field of common law. Scottish, Irish, Manx and Channel Island readers should be warned, therefore, but, with this caution in mind, they are recommended to read on, even if only for the purpose of extracting amusement from the quaint customs of their less-civilised brethren.

Even the law of England and Wales is going through a fundamental change with the advent of the Common Market. To the two traditional sources of Act of Parliament and the common law must now be added Community law, showing its influence in such widely varying fields as the proper additives to animal feeding stuffs and the requirement for horses to be measured in metric units for the purpose of the Horse Breeding Act. Community law has not yet made a significant impression on the subject of this book, although it is likely soon to do so, especially in connection with the unification of the laws on contractual terms and the export of horses.

Finally a word about the subject matter. In connection with damage done by animals it has been said that 'the law of torts has grown up historically in separate compartments . . . and beasts have travelled in a compartment of their own.' This might be true of one small aspect of the law but it is by no means generally correct. The law relating to horses cannot be compartmentalised in this way and no attempt will be made to do so. If a case relating to horses illustrates a general principle that case will be quoted, but if another general principle of interest to the horse owner is illustrated by a case relating to motor cars, then that case will be used. There is no law of horses as such, but there are many aspects of the broad spectrum of the law which affect horsemen and it is these aspects that the book seeks to highlight and bring together.

A startling example of non-compartmentalisation is contained in section 189 (1) of the Income and Corporation Taxes Act 1970 upon which claims for travelling expenses are based:

> 'If the holder of an office or employment is necessarily obliged to incur and defray out of the emoluments thereof the expenses of travelling in the performance of the duties of the office or employment or of keeping and maintaining a horse to enable him to perform the same . . . there may be deducted from the emoluments to be assessed the expenses so necessarily incurred and defrayed.'

If this section allows a company director to claim the expenses of keeping and maintaining his motor car against tax the writer feels at complete liberty to illustrate any legal principles contained in the book with equally apparently unconnected examples.

Chapter 1

LEARNING TO RIDE

THE CONTRACT

Legal perfection and real life are worlds apart. Consider the case of the first riding lesson. No trembling novice, with his heart in his mouth, would dream of discussing contractual terms with his tutor to be, yet this is what he ought to be doing because he is on the verge of entering into a contractual relationship. On one hand the riding school proprietor is contracting to teach the novice to ride and, on the other, the novice is agreeing to pay – but to pay for what? The fact that the proprietor has agreed to provide a service for reward creates a contract, but nine times out of ten the contract will be silent on every point likely to cause future difficulties.

Implied Terms

In the unreal world of legal perfection all foreseeable terms would be hammered out and, if not set down in writing, at least agreed verbally on the basis that verbal contracts are just as binding as written ones. The price would be agreed, as would the number and duration of lessons, the competence to be attained, the type of riding to be taught and the standard of horse to be provided. In the world in which real people take riding lessons, however, each side will wait until a difficulty arises and then look to the law to imply a term to cover the glaring gaps in their almost non-existent contract. Within limits the law does do this, but only reluctantly and only subject to very strict guidelines. The test can best be expressed in the words of Scrutton L.J.: 'A term can only be implied if it is necessary in the business sense to give efficacy to the contract, i.e. if it is such a term that it can be confidently said that if, at the time the contract was being negotiated, someone had said to the parties: "What will happen in such a case?" they would have replied: "Of course so and so will happen, we did not trouble to say that, it is too clear." '

Because of these guidelines very few terms will be implied into a contract to give riding lessons. Only three readily spring to mind, one to the effect that the instructor possesses and will exercise the appropriate skills, another that the horse provided is fit and sound for the purpose, being suited to the pupil's experience and riding skills, and the third that the horse is fitted with safe saddlery. If a beginner, who has made his lack of experience clear, is provided with a spirited, unmanageable horse which throws him, he will have a claim against the school for breach of an implied term, and similarly if his fall comes about from the slipping of a badly fitting saddle. In addition he will have a further claim if the instructor proves incapable of controlling his horses and conducting the lesson in a careful and safe manner.

Even fewer terms will be implied into a contract for the hire of a horse. Here the proprietor has not contracted to teach anything but has merely agreed to allow the rider to have the use of a horse in return for payment. In such a case there are two implied terms, one on the part of the proprietor, that the horse is suitable for the type of riding envisaged and the other, on the part of the rider, that he will take reasonable care of the horse and will return it at the end of the hiring in a condition consistent with that requirement. The rider should, therefore, make sure that he expressly specifies the purpose for which he requires the horse. If, for instance, he specifies he intends to hunt it he is entitled to expect that it is capable of jumping to a minimum standard, galloping and of generally behaving itself in the company of other horses. If he specifies he wants it for hacking and then takes a tumble whilst out hunting he will have no redress against the proprietor, even if the fall was brought about by the complete inability of the horse to take a fence. Indeed, in these circumstances, if the horse also falls and hurts itself, the proprietor will have a claim against the rider for breach of implied condition – *Burnard* v. *Haggis* (1863).

The liability of the rider to take reasonable care of the hired horse does not stop at taking care whilst riding. Care must be exercised during the whole time the animal is in his possession, so that if it falls ill it must either be returned to its owner, if the terms of the hiring allow, or a vet must be called at the hirer's expense. He runs a grave risk if he attempts to treat the animal himself for, if anything were to go wrong, the proprietor could claim there had been a breach of the implied condition in that reasonable care in the case of illness requires the summoning of a vet – *Deane* v. *Keate* (1811).

Express Terms

The lesson to be learnt from the foregoing is that if either side wishes to have any terms in the contract over and above those which are certain to be implied by law, or if they wish to modify the effect of any implied term, they should make such terms or modifications expressly part of the agreement between them. Usually, where express terms are included, they are included on the insistence of the proprietor as the pupil is seldom in a position to negotiate. The two most usual ones are a term requiring the hirer to be absolutely responsible for the safety of the horse and a term excluding the liability of the proprietor to the rider. The effect of this latter term will be examined later in the chapter but, in the absence of the former, if the hirer injures the horse in the hunting field in circumstances which are compatible with him having taken reasonable care of it, the proprietor will have no claim; that is, of course, if the horse was hired for the express purpose of hunting.

NEGLIGENCE

Primarily the legal relationship between the pupil or the hirer and the riding school is one of contract, so if any dispute arises they must both look to the terms of the contract for a solution. Usually, however, the contract will be silent on the point at issue and the implied terms will not cover the gap. In such a case the pupil or hirer is sometimes in a better position than the proprietor for he may be afforded some form of redress under the tort of negligence. In fact, even if there is an express or implied term in the contract, the same set of circumstances may give him a choice of proceeding under breach of contract or in negligence; so as the term negligence will crop up time and again in the following pages it may be appropriate to define it at this stage.

Essentials of Legal Negligence

There is currently a movement afoot to amend the law to provide that whenever someone is accidentally injured compensation automatically follows, whether or not the injury is caused by the fault of another. As the law stands at the moment, however, before compensation is awarded the courts require proof of some culpable act or omission on the part of some person other than the injured party and the compensation is then awarded in the form of a judgement for damages. In most personal injury cases this culpable act or omission will have to amount to negligence which, in legal terms, goes well beyond the everyday definition of careless conduct. For an injured party to succeed in negligence he must be able to show firstly that the other party owed him a duty of care, secondly that there has been a breach of that duty and finally that his injuries are a foreseeable result of that breach.

In the context of this chapter the first question to be answered is: Does a riding school proprietor owe a duty of care to his pupils and to those who hire his horses? – and the answer must be that he does. The second question of whether there has been a breach of that duty can only be answered by asking a further question: What standard of care has the proprietor to observe? If his conduct does not match that standard then there has been a breach of the duty. The required standard has come up for judicial interpretation on countless occasions, but its definition has not altered appreciably since that given in 1856 by Alderson B.: 'Negligence is the omission to do something which a reasonable man, guided upon those considerations which ordinarily regulate the conduct of human affairs, would do, or doing something which a prudent and reasonable man would not do.' In conjunction with this definition is the requirement that a man who holds himself out as being able to perform a service must show the skills normally possessed by others performing that service, leading to the consequence that it is no defence for a riding school proprietor to claim he had done his best to avoid an accident when the vast majority of proprietors, in the same circumstances, would in fact have avoided it.

The fields of most likely risk for the proprietor are the matching of the horse to the pupil, the safety of the saddlery and the supervision of the lesson or ride, with probably the most onerous being the duty to ensure that the pupil gets a horse he can manage. In *Hollman* v. *Ayling* (1970) an eighteen-year-old girl was provided with a pony described in the evidence as being a little more wilful and livelier than the rest. The girl had been riding for some time at the school in question so they were aware of her capabilities and considered her able to manage but, to make sure, she was expressly told of the pony's character. The pony bolted and threw the girl, who then sued. In their defence the proprietors relied firstly on their belief that the girl was sufficiently competent to manage her mount and secondly on the fact that they had given her a warning. Neither defence was successful and the girl was awarded damages. The result would presumably have been different had the pony been a normally quiet one which was suddenly frightened by some unusual noise or sight, and it might also have been different if the proprietors had not been so well aware of the girl's standard of competence. They were at fault in this case in knowing that the pony was headstrong and yet allowing a learner to ride it.

As well as providing suitable horses the proprietor must also take care to ensure that the ride is properly supervised. To take an extreme example, it would be risky in law for a proprietor to send out a string of complete novices under the control of only one experienced rider. There should be sufficient supervisors, both mounted and unmounted, to ensure that if more than one pony becomes frightened or unmanageable all of them can be brought under control. The ratio of supervisors to riders depends on many factors, not the least of which is the competence of the learners, but for the first few lessons one to one would not be unreasonable. For this reason it would be wise to arrange for all the pupils on any given ride to be roughly at the same level of experience. Not only does this make it easier to decide on the number of supervisors required, but it also ensures that no one is ever completely out of his depth. If a novice goes out with more experienced riders who decide to gallop, he might find himself involuntarily galloping if his horse decides to follow the others. If he falls off and injures himself the proprietor could face a claim for negligence and that claim might succeed on the grounds that the novice's limitations had not been properly taken into account.

Defences

There are, of course, defences open to a proprietor charged with negligence, the chief of which is that he had taken all reasonable precautions; in other words that he had not been negligent. If, after taking all reasonable precautions, some unforeseeable event intervenes this cannot amount to negligence. A proprietor can hardly be held responsible if he takes a ride on a quiet country lane, using well-behaved ponies and an adequate number of experienced supervisors, and a gunshot from an adjoining wood frightens the ponies. A claim against him by one of the riders who is thrown is hardly likely to succeed, although it might be different if the ride had been taken past a shooting range where the proprietor knew, or ought to have known, that firing would be taking place.

Another defence, or quasi-defence, is that of contributory negligence in which the defendant is found to be negligent but the plaintiff's damages are reduced because of his own contribution to his misfortunes. This is not a true defence as it implies that the defendant is guilty which is, of course, the negation of a defence, but it is highly important as it can have a considerable bearing on the damages awarded. Where contributory negligence applies the damages are apportioned in the ratio of the blameworthiness of each party, so if a rider is injured in circumstances which make him twenty-five per cent to blame for the accident, he will only be able to recover seventy-five per cent of the amount he would have been awarded had he been completely free from fault.

Contributory negligence has its limitations and it would not, for instance, be available in a case where the plaintiff's alleged negligent action occurred in the agony of the moment. The best known example of this limitation is the case of *Jones* v. *Boyce* (1816) in which the plaintiff was a passenger in a coach being negligently and furiously driven by the defendant. Fearing for his safety he jumped off and broke his leg. He commenced an action for damages only to find that the defendant was prepared to add insult to injury by claiming that his damages should be reduced because of the fact that if he had stayed on the coach he would have come to no harm. The court held, however, that the defendant's driving had put his passenger in the predicament of having to make a choice and the fact that the wrong choice might have been made in the heat of the moment could not amount to contributory negligence and therefore the damages would not be reduced. *Jones* v. *Boyce* can be equated with the case of a novice rider given a lively horse to ride and the horse bolts. It bolts in a straight line but the novice, whose skills should have enabled him to stay put, decides to jump off and is injured. In such a case it would be held that the damages arising out of the defendant's initial negligence in providing him with an unsuitable horse would not be reduced on a claim of contributory negligence based on the rider's action in 'baling out'. The rider might perhaps have made a wrong decision, but it was forced on him.

Somewhat akin to contributory negligence is the defence that the injured party, freely and voluntarily, with full knowledge of the nature and extent of the risk, impliedly agreed to incur it. Two contrasting cases illustrate the need for the risk to have been voluntarily undertaken. In *Haynes* v. *Harwood* (1935) a policeman was injured whilst trying to stop a runaway horse which had been negligently left unattended in a busy street. As his defence the owner of the horse claimed that the policeman's injuries arose from him voluntarily accepting the risk inherent in his action, but the defence failed as the court held that, because of his office and because of the danger to members of the public, the policeman had no choice other than to act as he did, therefore his action could not be said to be voluntary.

In the contrasting case of *Cutler* v. *United Dairies* (*London*) *Ltd* (1933) Mr Cutler, with the best of intentions, had entered a private field to assist in controlling an unruly horse which had escaped due to the negligence of its driver. The horse reared and threw him to the ground, causing serious injuries. On a claim for damages it was held that Mr Cutler had acted as he did without compulsion so he had voluntarily accepted the risk involved, unfortunately thereby ruling out any possibility of success in his action. The slightly regrettable lesson to be learned from these two cases would appear to be to mind one's own business, but it is fair to say that the decision in the Cutler case would probably have gone the other way if Mr Cutler's assistance had been directed towards preventing personal injury rather than just being generally helpful.

The foregoing paragraphs illustrate the fact that the riding school proprietor is highly vulnerable to negligence claims, yet although a very high standard of care is expected from him the solution is largely in his own hands. What is required is foresight. The proprietor should put himself in the position of that fictitious character, the passenger on the Clapham omnibus, who embodies, in the eyes of the judiciary, the epitome of reasonableness and, from his seat on the top-deck, he should ask himself whether he is conducting every facet of his business to ensure that everyone using his services does so with the maximum of safety and the minimum of risk. He should examine his operating methods with critical care to see what improvements can be made and he should then put those improvements in hand forthwith. Accidents will, of course, continue to happen but at less legal risk to himself.

OCCUPIER'S LIABILITY

The proprietor's self-examination should not be limited to the character of his horses, the safety of his saddlery and the competence of his staff, but should also extend to the condition of his premises. Since the Occupier's Liability Act of 1957 the occupier of premises is required to exercise such care (in the Act called 'the common duty of care') as in all the circumstances of the case is reasonable to see that the visitor to his premises is reasonably safe in using the premises for the purpose for which he is invited or permitted to be there. A person who comes to a riding school for lessons or to hire a horse is a visitor within this definition and if he is injured by some defect in the premises he will have a right of action. A hole in the surface of an exercise ring which causes a horse to stumble and throw its rider or a bare electric wire are both examples of actionable defects. The proprietor should examine his establishment to see if such flaws exist and, in deciding what to do about them, should consider the degree of care which would ordinarily be looked for in the type of visitor he gets. He is entitled to expect that his clients will be able to look after themselves up to a point, but some will be more vulnerable than others so it is these weaker brethren he should aim to protect. In particular he should be prepared for the fact that what might not present a danger to an adult could be a danger to a child, either because of the child's physical inability to cope with it, or because a child is not as aware of danger as an adult. By reason of this special duty of care to children, and because many of his pupils will be children, the 1957 Act places an onerous burden on the riding school proprietor.

EXCLUSION CLAUSES

Fortunately accidents seldom happen and, in case they do, they can be covered by insurance. The Riding Establishments Acts make it obligatory for adequate insurance to be carried but, in addition, many proprietors seek to avoid their liability, rather than insure against it, by the use of exclusion clauses. Even before the Unfair Contract Terms Act 1977 this was not easy and the Act has made it more difficult. An exclusion clause is a term in a contract whereby one party seeks to exclude his liability to the other for matters arising out of the contract, such as breach of a condition, and also for matters strictly outside the contract, such as negligence. Rather than being in any signed, written document they are frequently found in the form of notices – for example, 'Riders ride at their own risk'.

Prior to the 1977 Act a person who sought to rely on an exclusion clause was faced with two main difficulties. Firstly he had to prove that the clause was part of the contract and, as exclusion clauses frequently take the form of notices, this meant that he had to show that he had taken all reasonable steps to bring the notice to the other party's attention before the contract was concluded. In *Olley* v. *Marlborough Court Ltd* (1949) Mr and Mrs Olley booked in at an hotel and paid in advance at the reception desk. They went to their rooms where a notice was displayed relieving the hotel of any responsibility for loss of valuables not handed to the manageress for safe keeping. Mrs Olley's furs were stolen from the room in circumstances which indicated that the hotel had been negligent. She sued the hotel, but they sought to rely on the notice in the bedroom as a defence, claiming that it was a valid exclusion clause. It was held, however, that the contract had been made and completed at the reception desk, at which time the Olleys had no means of knowing of the notice, so it could not possibly have formed part of their contract. As it was not part of the contract the hotel could not rely on it. In the light of this case the riding school proprietor would do well to ensure that any exclusion notices are prominently displayed in the room or office in which he books in his customers.

The second difficulty was the one of construction. To be of effect the exclusion clause must be clear enough in its terms to show what liability it is excluding. Especially is this so when the defendant is trying to rely on such a clause to clear him of negligence. As he is using a contractual term to exclude a non-contractual liability the courts are very careful to make sure that the words of the clause do in fact exclude that liability. In *Collins* v. *Richmond Rodeo Riding Ltd* (1966) a novice hired a horse from the defendants. The horse was too frisky for him and ran away, throwing him in the process. There was adequate evidence of negligence and also of breach of the implied contractual term that the horse should be reasonably fit for its intended use, so the novice sued. The defendants relied on the fact that there were prominent signs about the premises reading: 'You enter premises and ride at your own risk,' and 'All riders using horses do so at their own risk.' The judge accepted that all reasonable steps had been taken to bring these notices to the plaintiff's attention so they formed an effective defence – but only in part. The notices were effective to exclude the defendant's contractual liability to provide a horse reasonably fit for its intended purpose, but the court held that they were not sufficiently clearly worded to exclude liability in negligence. To avoid this type of liability clear and unambiguous terms have to be used, which presumably means that the word 'negligence' has to be specifically included.

The above two difficulties still exist, but, in addition, the Unfair Contract Terms Act adds two more. The first is contained in section 2(1) and is more in the nature of a complete stonewall than a difficulty. By section 2 (1) clauses in contracts seeking to exclude liability for the negligent death or personal injury of another person are absolutely prohibited. As a result of this the type of notice found in the Richmond Rodeo case, even if amended to specifically refer to negligence, is no longer a valid defence in a personal injury case. The riding school proprietor can still exclude the remainder of his liability (i.e. other than for death and personal injury caused by negligence), but here he meets with the second difficulty in that any clause attempting to do this must satisfy the requirements of reasonableness contained in section 11. In other words an exclusion clause will be ineffective unless it is reasonable and section 11(1) provides that such a clause is reasonable if it is 'a fair and reasonable one to be included having regard to the circumstances which were or ought reasonably to have been in the contemplation of the parties when the contract was made.' The definition relies very much upon the interpretation of the word 'reasonable' and presumably the judge will ask himself, in applying section 11, whether the damage which has occurred is the type of damage both parties had in mind when they entered into the exclusion clause. If it is, then the clause is a reasonable one, but if it isn't it is void. Until precedent establishes some guidelines the future of even the limited form of exclusion clause is very much in the balance.

Up to now the main consideration has been relationships between individuals, defining rights and liabilities and pointing out where claims for damages may lie. Parliament has, however, concerned itself with the running of riding establishments in the Riding Establishments Acts of 1964 and 1970 and, as these Acts introduce a new concept, that of criminal liability, they are accorded the following chapter to themselves.

Chapter 2

THE RIDING ESTABLISHMENTS ACTS

The setting up and, to a large extent, the running of a riding establishment is governed by the combined effect of the Riding Establishments Acts of 1964 and 1970, both of which are applicable to England, Wales and Scotland, but neither to Northern Ireland. Their general effect is to provide that riding establishments can only be conducted under licence granted by the local authority which has to be satisfied that certain minimum standards are observed. The licences are annual ones, running for twelve months from the beginning of the day upon which they are granted, although the applicant has the right to ask for his licence to come into force one year after the date of grant. As an alternative the local authority has the power to grant a three-month provisional licence when it is not satisfied that it would be justified in granting a full licence. A provisional licence can be renewed for a further three months, but no longer.

DEFINITION OF RIDING ESTABLISHMENT

A riding establishment is defined as a business which keeps

horses for either or both of the following purposes: the purpose of their being let out on hire, or the purpose of their being used in providing, in return for payment, instruction in riding. Either a person or a limited company can keep a riding establishment and they are deemed to keep it at the premises where the horses are kept (premises in this context including land). The Acts do not apply to all stables, but only to those where horses are kept for the defined purposes, and it should be noted that the business element is essential. Under the statutory definition a pure livery stable does not need a licence, but the definition could include teaching stables where no riding facilities are available to the public. For instance, a licence would be required for an establishment where instruction is given in the form of demonstration by members of the staff, the reason being that the horses are used for the purpose of providing instruction even though never mounted by the pupils.

QUALIFICATION FOR A LICENCE

Not everyone is qualified to apply for a licence. No one under the age of eighteen can apply, nor can any person who, for the time being, is disqualified under any one of a number of enactments listed in section 1(2) of the 1964 Act. The types of disqualification mainly relate to offences concerned with the well-being of animals; thus a person who is disqualified from keeping a dog under the Protection of Animals (Cruelty to Dogs) Act and a person who is disqualified from keeping a pet shop under the Pet Animals Act are both debarred from applying for a licence as long as those disqualifications are in force. It goes without saying that anyone disqualified under the principal Acts cannot reapply whilst the disqualification lasts.

An applicant for a licence must not only be a qualified

person within the provisions of section 1(2), but he must also be able to satisfy the local authority that he is suitable and qualified within the provisions of section 1(4) as amended. In the 1964 Act this required him to be qualified and suitable, either by experience in the management of horses or otherwise, but the 1970 Act deleted the term 'or otherwise' and required him to be suitable and qualified, either by experience in the management of horses or by being the holder of an approved certificate or by employing in the management of the establishment a person so qualified. The approved certificates are the Assistant Instructor's Certificate, Instructor's Certificate and Fellowship, all of the British Horse Society, and the Certificate of Fellowship of the Institute of the Horse. There are provisions for additional certificates to qualify if the Secretary of State wishes to make an order to that effect.

CONDITIONS OF THE LICENCE

The Acts give the local authority complete discretion over whether to grant or refuse a licence, although an aggrieved applicant can appeal to a magistrates' court, both over the refusal and over any conditions the authority has imposed. The magistrates may then give such directions with respect to the issue of the licence or to the conditions as they think proper. Without prejudice to its discretion to withhold a licence on any grounds the authority has to take regard of the need to secure eight points listed in section 2 of the 1970 Act and the licence, if granted, must specify such conditions as it deems necessary or expedient in the particular case to ensure the securing of those points. The eight points are as follows and can be used as a guide by anyone, not merely the proprietor of a riding establishment, to the principles of good stable management:

(i) that paramount consideration will be given to the condition of horses and that they will be maintained in good health, and in all respects physically fit and that, in the case of a horse kept for the purpose of it being let out on hire for riding or a horse kept for the purpose of its being used in providing instruction in riding, the horse will be suitable for the purpose for which it is kept;

(ii) that the feet of all animals are properly trimmed and that, if shod, their shoes are properly fitted and in good condition;

(iii) that there will be available at all times, accommodation for horses suitable as respects construction, size, number of occupants, lighting, ventilation, drainage and cleanliness and that these requirements are complied with not only in the case of new buildings but also in the case of buildings converted for use as stabling;

(iv) that in the case of horses maintained at grass there will be available for them at all times during which they are so maintained adequate pasture, shelter and water and that supplementary feeds will be provided as and when required;

(v) that horses will be adequately supplied with suitable food and drink and (except in the case of horses maintained at grass, so long as they are so maintained) bedding material, and will be adequately exercised, groomed and rested and visited at suitable intervals;

(vi) that all reasonable precautions will be taken to prevent and control the spread amongst horses of infectious or contagious diseases and that veterinary first-aid equipment and medicines shall be provided and maintained within the premises;

(vii) that appropriate steps will be taken for the protection and extrication of horses in the case of fire and, in particular, that the name, address and telephone number of the licence holder or some other responsible person will be kept displayed in a prominent position on the outside of the premises and that instructions as to action to be taken in the event of fire, with particular regard to the extrication of horses, will be kept displayed in a prominent position on the outside of the premises;

(viii) that adequate accommodation will be provided for forage, bedding, stable equipment and saddlery.

It is clear from the section that the above eight points need not appear verbatim as conditions to the licence, in fact the local authority may even dispense with some of them if it thinks the circumstances warrant it. Whatever conditions it imposes in this respect, however, there are a further five mandatory conditions which must attach to the licence and these appear in section 2 of the 1970 Act. The mandatory conditions apply whether or not they are expressly specified and are as follows:

(i) a horse found on inspection of the premises by an authorised officer to be in need of veterinary attention shall not be returned to work until the holder of the licence has obtained at his own expense and has lodged with the local authority a veterinary certificate that the horse is fit for work;

(ii) no horse will be let out on hire for riding or used for providing instruction in riding without supervision by a responsible person of the age of sixteen years or over unless (in the case of a horse let out for hire for riding) the holder of the licence is satisfied that the hirer of the horse is competent to ride without supervision;

(iii) the carrying on of the business of a riding establishment shall at no time be left in the charge of any person under sixteen years of age;

(iv) the licence holder shall hold a current insurance policy which insures him against liability for any injury sustained by those who hire a horse from him for riding and those who use a horse in the course of receiving from him, in return for payment, instruction in riding and arising out of the use or hire of a horse as aforesaid and which also insures such person in respect of any liability which may be incurred by him in respect of any injury to any person caused by, or arising out of, the hire or use of a horse as aforesaid;

(v) a register shall be kept by the licence holder of all horses in his possession aged three years and under and usually kept on the premises which shall be available for inspection by an authorised officer at all reasonable times.

In connection with mandatory condition (v) it will be noted that the requirement to register relates to all horses kept on the premises and not just to those kept for riding or instruction. If, therefore, the licence holder keeps a horse for his own use, or at livery for some other person, it must be included in the register if it is three years old or under.

INSPECTION OF PREMISES

The local authority may itself, or through the agency of a veterinary surgeon or practitioner chosen from a list drawn up for that purpose by the Royal College of Veterinary

Surgeons and the British Veterinary Association, inspect and report on premises which are either the subject of a licence, the subject of an application for a licence or those on which it suspects an unlicensed riding establishment is being run. In the first and last cases the object of the inspection is to see if any offence is being committed, but in the case of an inspection of premises which are the subject of an application for a licence it will usually be in connection with the requirements of section 1(3) of the 1964 Act. By that section, where a local authority is considering an application, it is not to proceed to a decision until it has received and considered a report from a veterinary surgeon or practitioner containing sufficient detail to enable it to decide whether the premises are suitable and describing the condition of any horses found there.

The right of entry conferred by the Acts is rather worrying in its implications. Without a doubt the local authority should have the right to inspect licensed premises and also those it is considering licensing, but it appears to be an erosion of liberty to allow its representatives to inspect unlicensed premises merely on the suspicion of an offence being committed. Even the police need a search warrant in much more serious cases, and that the 1964 Act should confer greater powers than those possessed by the police on the local authority is a reflection on the current standing of the privacy of property. Especially is this so in the light of section 2(4) which makes it an offence to wilfully obstruct or delay an inspector, even if his inspection is being made on the flimsiest of suspicions.

OFFENCES CONNECTED WITH RIDING ESTABLISHMENTS

As well as the power to inspect, the local authority is given the power to take proceedings before magistrates if it thinks an offence has been committed. Any one of the following can give rise to a prosecution:

(a) the running of an unlicensed establishment;
(b) the running of an establishment in breach of a condition of the licence;
(c) at a time when a horse is in such a condition that its riding would be likely to cause suffering to the horse, the letting out of the horse on hire or using it for the purpose of providing, in return for payment, instruction in riding or for the purpose of demonstrating riding;
(d) the letting out on hire for riding or using for the purpose of providing, in return for payment, instruction in riding or for the purpose of demonstrating riding any horse aged three years or under or any mare heavy with foal or any mare within three months after foaling;
(e) supplying for a horse which is let out on hire for riding, equipment which is used in the course of the hiring and suffering, at the time when it is supplied, from a defect of such a nature as to be apparent on inspection and as to be likely to cause suffering to the horse or an accident to the rider;
(f) failing to provide such curative care as may be suitable, if any, for a sick or injured horse which is kept with a view to its being let out on hire or used for a purpose mentioned in paragraph (c);
(g) keeping a riding establishment and knowingly permitting any person, who is for the time being disqualified under the Act from keeping a riding establishment, to have control or management of the keeping of the establishment;

(h) with intent to avoid inspection under section 2 of the 1964 Act, concealing or causing to be concealed any horse maintained by the riding establishment.

The above list is not exhaustive but it gives the main offences under the two Acts, the majority of which are contained in section 3 of the 1964 Act. One interesting point to emerge from the list is that the offence in paragraph (e) seems designed to protect a person who hires a horse but not a person who takes instruction on a horse. Throughout the Act these two persons have been meticulously separated and, in general, given the same protection, but when it comes to defective saddlery the latter has been left out.

Conviction for any of the above offences can lead to a fine not exceeding £50, but it can also lead to an order cancelling the licence and disqualifying the offender from keeping a riding establishment for such period as the magistrates think fit. These sanctions are criminal in nature and, because of this, the offences are prosecuted by the state through the agency of the local authority. Subject to what is said later, criminal offences do not, of themselves, give rise to a right for civil damages, so a party injured by a proven criminal act does not automatically recover compensation, and will not usually do so unless he can prove that there has also been a civil wrong. Take, for instance, the offence under the 1964 Act of hiring out a horse with defective equipment. This is a criminal offence and the hirer can be prosecuted under section 3(1)(b), whether or not the rider is injured. If the rider is injured, however, his action for damages will not be based on section 3(1)(b), but on the civil tort of negligence. The criminal prosecution and the civil action will be founded on exactly the same facts, but their outcome will be different.

STATUTORY DUTY

Having made this general point, however, there does appear to be some ground for thinking that offences against certain sections of the Riding Establishments Acts can form the basis of a civil claim in themselves, based on the concept of breach of statutory duty. For some years, especially in connection with statutes relating to the safety of workmen, the courts have been developing a form of action which indicates that they regard certain laws which protect the public interest as also protecting the private individual. This cause of action is still very limited in its application but there would appear to be no reason, for instance, why a civil claim should not be based on a breach of the mandatory condition requiring rides to be supervised by responsible persons of the age of sixteen years and over. Fortunately this grey area may never need to be explored as the tort of negligence is so far-reaching that the facts giving rise to a prosecution under the Acts are more than likely also to amount to negligence.

Chapter 3

ACQUIRING PREMISES

To deal with the subject matter of this chapter Hill and Redman's *Landlord and Tenant* takes over two thousand pages, *Emmet on Title* takes an additional one thousand two hundred and the *Encyclopedia of Town and Country Planning* uses no less than four loose-leaf volumes. Obviously, therefore, pruning on a massive scale is necessary, so the plan will be to outline the law in a very general manner but to give rather more detail on points of interest to the horse owner seeking to acquire grazing land or stables.

AGISTMENT

Acquisition of premises can take two forms: buying or leasing; but before progressing to these it may be worth considering agistment as a temporary, or even permanent, method of keeping a horse. Agistment is an arrangement whereby the owner of land takes another's animals to graze on his land for reward. The payment is usually calculated on a weekly basis and the arrangement differs fundamentally from a lease or a tenancy in that the animal owner acquires no interest in the land. The land owner has a duty to take reasonable care of his charges and he is liable for any injury caused to them by his negligence. Three cases illustrate the point:

In *Smith* v. *Cook* (1875) the landowner ran an agisted horse with some heifers in a field next to one containing a bull. The division between the two fields was a shallow ditch and he knew that from time to time the bull had crossed over to be with the heifers. This happened again and the bull injured the horse. It was held that the land owner had not taken proper care of the horse and damages were awarded against him. The case of *Turner* v. *Stallibras* (1898) shows that the land owner's duty extends to making sure there are no dangerous pitfalls on his land. He was here held liable in damages when an agisted horse was caught up in, and injured by, barbed wire hidden in long grass. The third case, *Halestrap* v. *Gregory* (1895), demonstrates that the land owner may still be liable, even if the actual damage is caused by a third party, if the original negligence was his. In this case the defendant's servant negligently left a gate open, allowing a horse which his employer was agisting to stray onto adjoining land. The owner of the adjoining land tried to drive the horse back through the gate, but unfortunately it fell over a fence and was injured. Despite the fact that he had nothing to do with the immediate cause of the injury, the defendant was ordered to pay damages as the accident was the natural result of the open gate.

The horse's owner is entitled to take back the horse on demand and the land owner cannot retain it, even as security for unpaid money due for the grazing. His only means of recovering the arrears is to sue in debt. He does, however, have a certain interest in the animal, sufficient at least for him to sue in conversion, defined as an action protecting the plaintiff's interest in the dominion and control of a chattel. Thus, if a third party takes the horse out of the field and rides it, the land owner has the necessary interest in the animal to enable him to recover damages.

LEASE OR TENANCY

Agistment may prove to be useful but, in due course, the horse owner will want to have land of his own. As a purchase might be too expensive in the initial stages of his interest, he may consider taking a tenancy or a lease, both being preferable to agistment as they give the tenant the sole and exclusive use of the land. The choice between the two depends very much upon which the landlord is prepared to offer but, from the tenant's point of view, the latter is probably preferable as it gives a fixed period of occupancy, usually longer than the security of tenure afforded by a periodic tenancy.

A periodic tenancy is created by an agreement which gives the tenant exclusive right to the use and occupancy of premises for a periodic term, such as from week to week, or year to year. The tenancy is usually expressed to be determinable by either party giving the other an agreed length of notice but, in default of agreement, the law requires six months' notice, expiring at the end of a year of the tenancy, for a year-to-year period, and notice equal at least to a period of the tenancy for any other. In default of express stipulation, the method of identifying the period of the tenancy is by the rent intervals. A tenancy of £*x* per month is a monthly tenancy, but a tenancy at £*y* per year with rent payable by monthly instalments of £*x* is a yearly tenancy. The former would require at least one month's notice to quit, and the latter six months' notice.

The disadvantages of a periodic tenancy can readily be seen. To alter the rent the landlord has only to serve, or threaten to serve, the appropriate notice to terminate and then renegotiate a new rent as a condition of continuing the term. No doubt market forces put a ceiling on the increase, but the tenant is tempted to pay over the going rate to avoid the upheaval of moving. Subject to these market forces the landlord can ask for increases as often as he likes, so the tenant can never feel justified in making improvements because the landlord may use those improvements as an argument for increasing the rent, and also because the tenancy may be brought to an end before he has had any benefit out of the expenditure. Parliament has partially recognised these disadvantages and has provided varying degrees of security of tenure, but only to tenants of dwelling-houses, agricultural holdings and business premises. Unfortunately, private horse owners are not included amongst the protected classes, although the riding school proprietor and the stud farmer may obtain some benefit from the Agricultural Holdings Acts, and substantial benefit from the business tenancy provisions of the Landlord and Tenant Act 1954.

Agricultural Tenancies

As these Acts give some security of tenure and a certain amount of rent control it is worth enquiring who can claim their protection, beginning with the Agricultural Holdings Act of 1948 as amended by the Agricultural Holdings (Notices to Quit) Act of 1977. Security of tenure under the Acts is given to the tenant of an agricultural holding, defined as the aggregate of the agricultural land comprised in a contract of tenancy. Agricultural land is land used for agriculture and agriculture is expressed to include livestock breeding and using land for grazing and as meadow. So far the definition suggests that a field let for the keeping of a weekend pony qualifies as an agricultural holding, but unfortunately the 1948 Act goes on to provide that not only must the land be used for agriculture but that it must also be so used for the purposes of a trade or business, although the trade or business need not necessarily be connected with agriculture. This point came to be considered in 1962, in the case of *Rutherford* v. *Maurer*. The owner of a field let it to the proprietor of a riding school for grazing purposes only, then attempted to repossess it by serving a six months' notice to quit. The proprietor claimed she had an agricultural tenancy entitling her to twelve months' notice and to the protection of the 1948 Act. In the County Court she was defeated, but she took the case to the Court of Appeal where a decision was given in her favour. The appeal judges accepted that the field was used for an agricultural purpose as it was used for grazing within the definition contained in the Act. They also found that the field was not only used for agriculture, but was so used for the purposes of a trade or business, albeit not an agricultural one. They held that the County Court judge had been wrong in deciding that the trade or business must be one of agriculture as the definition in the Act was sufficiently wide to allow any sort of trade or business, including that of a riding school, to be included.

An interesting case to consider in conjunction with *Rutherford* v. *Maurer* is the rating case of *Young* (*V.O.*) v. *West Dorset District Council* (1977) in which the rating position of seventy-nine acres of pastureland attached to a riding stable and used for grazing the stable's horses, fell to be considered. Under the relevant legislation, agricultural land is exempt from rates but not if it is kept or preserved mainly or exclusively for purposes of sport or recreation.

The Land Tribunal had to decide whether the pastureland in this case was ratable, with the rating authority arguing that it was on the grounds that its ultimate use was for keeping horses for sport or pleasure. The Tribunal found against the authority, however, and decided that the ultimate use was irrelevant, the only matter of concern being the actual use and, as the land was used for grazing, the actual use was agricultural.

Rutherford's case relates to a field let to a riding school, but what of the letting of the riding school itself? Can the tenancy of a riding school, including its stables, exercise yard and grazing land be held to constitute an agricultural tenancy? The answer is probably not, based upon the fact that the test for determining whether mixed premises make an agricultural holding is the one of dominant or main use. As the dominant or main use of a riding school is not agricultural, a tenancy of one cannot be agricultural, even though it includes agricultural components, such as grazing land and meadow land. In *Re Joel's Lease* (1930) a similar question was considered in relation to a stud farm used principally for the breeding of racehorses. The court ruled against the tenancy of such a farm being an agricultural one as agriculture was not its main purpose, but, at first sight, this decision seems surprising as the Agricultural Holdings Act specifically includes the breeding of livestock in the definition of agriculture. When the statutory meaning of livestock is considered, however, it becomes clear that racehorses do not qualify: 'Livestock includes any creature kept for the production of food, wool, skins or fur, or for its use in the farming of land or the carrying on in relation to land of any agricultural activity.'

As Rutherford's case shows that under certain circumstances the Agricultural Holdings Acts can apply to horsemen, a brief summary of the protection they afford might be of use. The 1948 Act deals with liability for repairs, insurance and compensation for improvements, but its main effect is upon the security of tenure which an agricultural holding gives to tenants. The security sections have now been re-enacted and extended by the Agricultural Holdings (Notices to Quit) Act of 1977 so, unless otherwise stated, the following references will be to the 1977 Act.

The first obvious benefit of an agricultural tenancy is that twelve months' notice expiring at the end of a year of the tenancy is required to terminate it. This contrasts favourably with the more normal six months' notice, but even a twelve months' notice is unlikely to end an agricultural tenancy as the tenant has the right to serve a counter-notice within one month, unless the landlord's notice was served upon one of the grounds specified in section 2(3). The service of the counter-notice has the effect of making the landlord's notice ineffective and, if he wishes to proceed further, he must obtain the consent of the Agricultural Land Tribunal to its operation. The Tribunal must give its consent if satisfied of the existence of one or more of the grounds specified in section 3(3), unless it appears to them that in the circumstances a fair and reasonable landlord would not insist on possession. The grounds contained in section 3(3) relate, very generally, to whether the termination of the tenancy would be desirable in the interests of good husbandry and good farm management, or whether refusal of consent would cause greater hardship than granting it.

The consent of the Agricultural Land Tribunal is only required if the landlord's notice is not served on one of the grounds set out in section 2(3). If it is so served, and expressly says so, the tenant's counter-notice will have no effect. The reader is referred to the Act for details of the grounds, but amongst the more important are the following: that the land is required for a non-agricultural purpose for which planning permission has been given or for which permission is not necessary; that a bad husbandry certificate has been given by the Agricultural Land Tribunal; that the tenant has failed to comply with a notice requiring him to pay arrears of rent within two months; that the tenant, being the sole or the sole surviving tenant, has died and the notice is served within three months of his death. In this latter case qualified members of the deceased tenant's family have the right to apply for a succession to the tenancy.

Grazing Agreements

Obviously a landlord will think twice before granting an agricultural tenancy, but the 1948 Act provides for a type of tenancy which does not have the same difficulties over security. This is the letting of land for grazing or mowing during a specified period of the year, such as from April to October. The letting is for one season only and must be specifically renewed for the following season, in other words there is no continuity of tenure from season to season and the tenant has no rights other than for the current period. The Agricultural Holdings Acts do not apply to such lettings.

Business Tenancies

The stud-farm tenancy in *Re Joel's Lease* was held not to be an agricultural holding, but there is no doubt that it would today be classified as a business tenancy and so entitled to the protection of the Landlord and Tenant Act 1954, as amended by the Law of Property Act 1969. Like the Agricultural Holdings Acts, the 1954 Act is not solely concerned with security of tenure, but security is one of its most important provisions. The Act relates to premises occupied by a tenant, either wholly or partly, for his business under the provisions of a tenancy or lease. It does not apply to a term certain of six months or less, unless there is a provision for renewal beyond six months, or unless the tenant has been in occupation for a period which, together with any period of occupation by a predecessor in the business, exceeds twelve months. Business premises need not necessarily be buildings, as shown by the case of *Bracey* v. *Read* (1963) in which gallops on Farncombe Down and Crow Down near Lambourn were held to be premises with the effect that a tenancy of them by a racehorse trainer was a business tenancy within the 1954 Act.

A tenancy or lease within the 1954 Act, as amended, does not come to an end unless terminated in accordance with the provisions laid down. Even a lease for a fixed period does not terminate at the end of that period and continues until the landlord serves a notice under the Act requiring the term to be ended not more than twelve months and not less than six months from the date of service. There are two alternative forms of notice, one stating that the landlord would not oppose an application to the court for a new tenancy, and the other stating that he would oppose such an application. If the latter form is used it must set out the grounds contained in section 30 of the 1954 Act upon which the opposition would be made. The tenant has two months within which to inform the landlord whether he intends to give up the tenancy. If he serves this counter-notice he can then apply to the court for a new tenancy, but if he does not, his existing tenancy comes to an end on the expiry of the landlord's notice.

Once again the reader is referred to the Act for the exact grounds of opposition under section 30 but, briefly, three of them arise out of the tenant's default, such as failure to carry out repair obligations, persistent delay in paying rent and substantial breach of other obligations under the lease or tenancy agreement. A fourth ground is that the landlord will provide suitable alternative accommodation, another that the landlord intends to carry out substantial demolition or reconstruction work which he cannot do with the tenant in possession, and another that at the end of the tenancy he intends to occupy the premises for his own business or as his residence.

The statutory notice cannot bring a fixed term to an end, but can only serve to determine the occupation when the fixed term has expired. Thus a lease for three years runs for three years and thereafter it continues until the requisite notice is served, although the notice can be served six months before the end of the three-year term to bring it to an end at its expiry. On an unopposed application to the court, or upon an unsuccessfully opposed application, the court can grant a new tenancy for a period which it considers reasonable in the circumstances at the current market rent.

Fixed-Term Leases

We have seen that the agricultural tenant is protected and the business tenant is protected, so under one or another of these heads protection is afforded to the riding school proprietor, the stud farmer, the livery stable and the race-horse trainer. The private horse owner, however, who uses his horse merely for pleasure, is left at his landlord's mercy. His protection is to attempt to obtain a lease for a fixed period of years, so giving himself the opportunity to plan ahead and decide whether any expenditure on improvements is worthwhile. A lease differs from a periodic tenancy in that it is expressed to be for a fixed term, usually calculated in a number of years, and comes to an end at the termination of that term without the necessity of a notice to quit. The landlord cannot end the term during its currency unless the lease has given him an express power to do so, or unless he has reserved a right of re-entry on the happening of certain events, such as the tenant's failure to pay the rent or the breach of a condition. Even if there is such a power of re-entry the tenant has a statutory right to apply to the court for relief against the forfeiture of the lease and, in the case of re-entry (or forfeiture) for non-payment of rent, relief can even be granted for a period of six months after the landlord has re-possessed. Thus if the landlord takes possession on the grounds of rent arrears the tenant may, within a period of six months thereafter, apply to the court to have himself restored into possession of the premises. Naturally he will be required to pay off the arrears and pay to the landlord any expenses incurred.

Although the advantages of a lease over a tenancy are obvious its terms should be carefully considered before acceptance. It may, for instance, prove expensive for a tenant to agree to keep old buildings in repair because, although he will not be required to modernise them or bring them up to date, he may find himself in the position of having to replace them piece by piece to perform his repairing obligations. He should also bear in mind the question of insurance, for if the premises are burnt down, a covenant to keep in repair would oblige him to rebuild. It is usual for the landlord to agree to repair the main walls, roof and main timbers, but this is by no means universal and responsibility for repairs depends upon the wording of the lease. If a tenant accepts a covenant obliging him to repair this requires him to keep the premises in a state of substantial repair having regard to their age and nature.

Even though security of tenure is comforting, the tenant should not forget that it cuts both ways. If he takes a five-year lease this means that he is bound by the obligations of that lease for five years, even if he loses interest in horses after two years and wants to give up his lease. He should make sure, therefore, that the lease contains no express or implied conditions preventing him from assigning or sub-letting. For instance his lease may contain a provision to the effect that the buildings can be used only for the stabling of horses. This may be perfectly acceptable at the beginning of the term, but if the tenant wishes to sell the lease his market is limited by that condition, unless he can persuade his landlord to alter it. Depending upon the demand for stabling, such a covenant may make the lease difficult or impossible to dispose of. Rather more obviously restrictive is a covenant expressly preventing assignment or sub-letting. If the landlord attempts to include such a covenant the tenant should insist that it be qualified by the words 'without the landlord's consent'. If the landlord then tries to refuse consent he will have to give a good reason for his refusal and in the absence of such a reason the tenant will be able to proceed without the consent. A covenant against assigning or sub-letting is not broken by agisting another person's animals on the land.

If the tenant falls into arrears with his rent the landlord may be able to re-possess the premises under a forfeiture clause, but he also has two other remedies, either to sue or to distrain. The landlord's right of distress is heavily circumscribed with legal conditions but, in essence, it is the right for himself, or a bailiff acting under a distress warrant, to enter upon the demised premises to take and sell chattels (including horses) to the amount of the rent in arrear and the costs of the distraint. The consequences of this are quite serious, not just for the tenant, but for a third party who has left his horses on the tenant's land as distress is not solely confined to the tenant's own chattels. The subject of agistment comes into question here, for if a horse is agisted on land held by a tenant and that tenant falls into arrears with his rent, the landlord may distrain on the horse, leaving the owner with a presumably valueless claim for damages against the tenant. The matter is not quite as serious if the tenancy is an agricultural holding within the meaning of the Agricultural Holdings Act 1948, for section 19 of the Act provides that the landlord can only take an agisted animal if there are not enough other chattels on the land to meet the amount of the debt.

PURCHASE

Agistment, tenancies and leases all have problems, so, in due course, the horse owner will probably consider purchasing premises. This subject will be touched upon only briefly as it is one on which professional guidance should be obtained at every step. There are some points, however, which the horse-owning purchaser should specifically check with his solicitor. For instance, freehold property, like leasehold property, can be subject to clauses restricting its uses. These are known as restrictive covenants, one of the more common ones being that premises should not be used for business purposes. If the intention of a purchaser is to start a riding school, such a covenant would be very unwelcome and might be serious enough to persuade him not to proceed. The solicitor should also be asked to check that there are legally enforceable rights of way to the premises and that the premises have rights of drainage, rights of water and rights to take electricity cables to them. As these rights are often exercised across land owned by a third party it is essential to see that they have been properly granted or acquired by long use. A particularly important point, as will be seen later in connection with the Animals Act 1971, is to be absolutely sure who is responsible for fencing. The liability for fencing can have important consequences in connection with damage done by straying animals, so it is a wise precaution to have the liability pin-pointed from the start.

TOWN AND COUNTRY PLANNING

Another important point to be borne in mind before signing the contract is the Town and Country Planning Act position. It is no use buying an otherwise ideally suitable property to find that the planning authority will not allow it to be used for the purpose for which it was acquired. No difficulty arises if there is no intention to build or to change the existing established use, but if, for instance, the stables and outbuildings of an old house are bought for the purpose of turning them into a riding school, an application for planning consent will be necessary and it would be prudent to make the contract conditional upon such consent being forthcoming.

Town planning has existed for very many years, but in its present form it dates from the Town and Country Planning Act 1947 now consolidated, with the intervening legislation, into the Town and Country Planning Act 1971. The essence of the system is that any development on land requires planning consent, subject to many exceptions. Development is defined as:

(a) the carrying out of building operations, engineering operations, mining operations or other operations in, on, over or under land; or
(b) the making of any material change in the use of any buildings or other land.

To build a stable, therefore, is classified as development under paragraph (a) and to change the use of private stabling to a riding school is development under (b), both operations requiring planning consent.

One of the afore mentioned exceptions which operates in favour of a private horse owner is that contained in section 22(2)(d) of the 1971 Act. By that section the use of any buildings or other land within the curtilage of a dwelling-house for any purpose incidental to the enjoyment of a dwelling-house as a dwelling-house, does not constitute development. By the same Act interior or exterior alterations to a building which do not materially affect the external appearance of the building do not constitute development. Using these two exceptions a stable could be made out of an existing outhouse or garage without the necessity of planning consent. This does not mean that a stable can be built, but only that existing buildings can be converted for that purpose.

There is, however, a provision contained in section 3 and the First Schedule to the Town and Country Planning General Development Order 1977 which allows the building of a totally new stable without planning consent. The provision states that no consent is required for:

'The enlargement, improvement or other alteration of a dwelling-house so long as:

(a) the cubic content of the original dwelling-house (as ascertained by external measurement) is not exceeded by more than 50 cubic metres or one tenth, whichever is the greater, subject to a maximum of 115 cubic metres;
(b) the height of the building as so enlarged, altered or improved does not exceed the height of the highest part of the roof of the original dwelling-house;
(c) no part of the building as so enlarged, altered or improved projects beyond the forwardmost part of any wall of the original dwelling-house which fronts on a highway.

Provided that the erection of a garage, stable, loose-box or coach-house within the curtilage of the dwelling-house shall be treated as the enlargement of the dwelling-house for all purposes of this permission including the calculation of cubic contents.'

By virtue of this provision a new stable or loose-box could be built as an enlargement to an existing house without planning permission, provided the conditions as to size and situation are observed.

Because of section 22(2)(e) of the 1971 Act the use of land for the purposes of agriculture is not classed as development, with the result that no permission is required to use land for agriculture, whatever its former use might have been. Unfortunately it was decided in *Belmont Farm Ltd* v. *Minister of Housing and Local Government* (1962) that the breeding and training of horses for show-jumping was not agriculture, so the use of land for that purpose required planning permission. Although the definition of agriculture contained in section 290 does include the keeping and breeding of livestock it was held that so far as horses are concerned, to qualify as livestock for planning purposes, they must be kept and bred for use in farming the land. Whereas Shire horses might qualify under this section, show-jumping horses do not.

Chapter 4

ACQUIRING A HORSE

BORROWING A HORSE

Like the acquisition of premises the acquisition of a horse can take the form of borrowing (akin to leasing) or of buying. Chapters 1 and 2 have touched upon the subject of borrowing for reward, but it may be useful to deal briefly with gratuitous borrowing, covering the situation where a friend lends a horse without payment. The borrower's obligations in such a case are thought to be exceptionally onerous, although there appears to be little relevant case law. Dealing with the matter on a theoretical level Halsbury's *Laws of England* suggests that the borrower is liable for the slightest degree of negligence and is bound to exercise the utmost amount of care. He must also, of course, return the horse to its owner on demand.

In the absence of agreement the borrower is responsible for the cost of feeding and for veterinary expenses whilst the horse is in his care, and he will also be responsible for damage caused by it to third parties. He must use the horse only for the particular purpose for which it is lent, so that if it is injured whilst being used for any other purpose he will be liable in damages. In the words of Holt C.J. in *Coggs* v. *Bernard* (1703): 'If a man should lend another a horse to go westward or for a month, if the borrower go northward or keep the horse above a month, if any accident happen to the horse in the northern journey, or after the expiration of the month, the borrower will be chargeable.'

On the other side the lender has the duty to make known to the borrower any defects or vices which might make the horse dangerous, but only to the extent of his own actual knowledge, and only to the extent that those vices would affect the use for which the horse is expressly lent. Thus if a pony is likely to rear when ridden but is lent for the purpose of pulling a trap, the borrower would not be able to recover damages for injuries received from a fall due to rearing whilst the pony was being ridden. This would be so even if the lender knew of the vice and had not passed his knowledge on. So far as he was concerned the pony was lent for trap work and if the borrower operated outside this understanding he did so completely at his own risk.

BUYING A HORSE – *caveat emptor*

In the absence of good friends willing to lend a horse as and when required it will be the ambition of most riders to buy their own. Despite horror stories centred on the evil ways of the horse dealer there is no mystery about the transaction. The buying and selling of horses is exactly the same as the buying and selling of any other type of goods, with the party who can keep his head and remember simple rules generally coming to no harm. The first rule for the buyer is the ancient one of *caveat emptor*, or let the buyer beware. Its significance stems from the fact that a purchaser is presumed to know exactly what he is buying and if he later finds out that he was mistaken, or that his purchase suffers from some defect of which he was not aware, then the loss falls on him without right of redress against the vendor. The full impact of this situation has been softened somewhat by legislation, but the law of the land is not yet so consumer orientated as to make it safe to ignore the rule.

Caveat emptor leads to the position that the purchaser of a horse has three choices: he may rely on his own skill and judgement in assessing his purchase; he may have the horse professionally examined and tested before buying so that he can sue the examiner if he proves to have made a mistake; or he may insist that the vendor gives a condition or a warranty as to soundness, freedom from vice, or as to any other quality which he, the purchaser, is looking for. The vendor can, of course, refuse an inspection or decline to enter into the required terms, but this should immediately put the purchaser on his guard.

Conditions and Warranties

Of the three choices the first one requires no elaboration as the buyer who makes this choice will be completely at risk; the second one will be considered later in the chapter, leaving the third to be analysed in some detail. In the first instance the difference between a condition and a warranty should be noted as the breach of either one or the other can lead to differing results. On the one hand breach of a condition can entitle the purchaser to repudiate the contract and obtain refund of his money plus expenses but, on the other, breach of a warranty only gives rise to a claim for damages. In a horse purchase agreement the effect of this is that a breach of condition by the vendor entitles the purchaser to return the horse and be restored to the *status quo ante* by return of his money and any costs involved, whilst on the breach of a warranty he cannot return the horse but can claim monetary damages for any loss the breach may have caused him.

In some cases the purchaser may be better suited by a breach of condition and, in others, by a breach of warranty, but his remedy is only open to choice when a condition has been broken, in which case he may elect to treat the condition as a warranty. It is not open to him to elect to treat a warranty as a condition. If he wishes to pursue the breach of condition by repudiating the contract he must act quickly, as delay may take the election out of his hands and convert the condition into a warranty by operation of law. In *Collins* v. *Martin-Bird* (1963) a horse had been bought subject to a condition that it was quiet in every way. Unfortunately it proved to be far from quiet in traffic but, instead of returning it immediately and claiming his money back, the purchaser attempted to cure the vice. After twenty-six weeks, when he found he was having no success, he tried to return the animal but the court held that the delay had been too long, although it was acknowledged that his right to claim damages remained unimpaired.

The obvious next step is to define conditions and warranties so they can be recognised on sight, but this is easier said than done. The Sale of Goods Act 1893 helps a little by saying that a warranty is a stipulation collateral to the main purpose of the contract. By combining that definition with decided cases it becomes clear that the difference lies in the intention of the parties. If they intend the term to be fundamental to the very existence of the contract then it is a condition, but if they intend it to be important but collateral to the main purposes (in other words the contract can stand without it) then it is a warranty. The difference is well illustrated by the case of *Harling* v. *Eddy* (1951). A vendor had put a cow up for auction and verbally stated at the time of the sale: 'I absolutely guarantee her and am willing to take her back if she proves as not stated.' The cow had been described in the sale particulars as T.T. but she subsequently turned out to have been suffering from tuberculosis at the time of the auction. The purchaser sued and the court had to decide whether the vendor's words were a condition or a warranty. The judge decided in favour of the former. He felt that the words 'I absolutely guarantee her', on their own, probably constituted a warranty, but the offer to take her back indicated that the vendor had intended to go beyond a warranty and enter into a condition. As a warranty gives the purchaser no right to return defective goods, the fact that the vendor, in this case, had expressed a willingness to take them back led to the conclusion that a condition had been intended.

In an earlier case, *Head* v. *Tattersall* (1871), the vendor guaranteed that the horse he sold had been hunted with the Bicester hounds. Here again this was probably a warranty as such a guarantee would normally be regarded as collateral to the main purpose of the contract, but the vendor also said that the horse could be returned the following Wednesday if it did not answer the description. The purchaser found out that it had not been hunted with the Bicester and brought proceedings in which the court upheld his right to return the horse within the time limit and recover his money, and this was despite the fact that in the intervening period it had been injured.

Breach of Warranty

The majority of contractual terms will amount to warranties rather than conditions and the importance of the former can be judged from the considerable amount of case law which has grown up concerning them over the years. Most of the relevant cases date back to the nineteenth century and beyond but, as warranties are still used and relied upon, the subject is worth further consideration. The first point to be noted is that no special words are needed to constitute a warranty, although those used must be near enough in time to the sale contract to form part of it. In the case of *Hopkins* v. *Tanqueray* (1854) an owner sent his horse to Tattersalls to be sold without warranty. A Mr Hopkins was examining it on the day before the sale when the owner saw him and said: 'You have nothing to look for, I assure you it is sound in every respect.' Hopkins accepted this assurance and bid successfully on the following day but later the horse proved to be unsound. Hopkins sued and it was held that he was unable to rely on the owner's statement as a warranty as it had been made too long before the actual purchase for it to have been part of the contract. The court also doubted whether it was possible for a private warranty to be given at a public auction.

The nature of a warranty is an undertaking by the vendor that the horse possesses the attributes he claims for it, or is free from the defects warranted against. The operative effective time of the warranty is the point of sale, so if a defect originates thereafter the vendor has no liability. The wording can, however, extend the protection to cover defects arising after the sale, but to do this the intention must be very clearly expressed. In *Chapman* v. *Gwyther* (1866) the words 'warranted sound for one month' came to be considered in this context, with the result that the court decided the true interpretation was that the horse was warranted sound at the time of sale but the purchaser only had one month from then in which to claim for a breach. The wording did not indicate that the purchaser was protected against unsoundness arising after the date of sale.

If a vendor gives a warranty his actual knowledge of the defect is usually immaterial. If he warrants a horse sound when it possesses a fault of which he was not aware, he will, nonetheless, be liable under his warranty. To avoid this situation he can incorporate such words as – 'so far as I am aware' – and by this means he can ensure he runs no risk of damages for defects outside his knowledge at the time of sale.

As long ago as 1471 it was decided that a purchaser could not use a warranty to claim damages for defects which were obvious. In 1616 Brian J. reaffirmed this in beautifully succint terms: 'To warrant a thing that may be perceived by sight is not good.' Because of this long-standing rule it is not open for a purchaser to buy a horse with only one eye and then sue the vendor under a warranty of soundness. There are, however, limitations, mainly based upon the fact that the defect must be truly obvious. For instance, if the purchase is completed over the telephone, with the buyer never having seen the horse, he would be able to rely on a warranty of soundness in the face of even the most obvious of defects, and if the warranty was given for the purpose of persuading the purchaser not to inspect, again it would hold good, even if an inspection would have revealed the fault.

As previously mentioned, no particular form of wording is needed to constitute a binding warranty, nor need it be in writing, although writing, even if only on the back of the receipt for the purchase money, does facilitate proof in the case of a dispute. The time-honoured expression 'Warranted sound and free from vice' is the one most usually encountered, but it is far from being the only one to have been recognised by the courts. In *Cave* v. *Coleman* (1828) the statement 'You may depend upon it that the horse is perfectly quiet and free from vice' was held to be a warranty even though the word 'warrant' had not been used. If the word is used, however, careful consideration is required to decide which part of a statement is a warranty and which mere description. In *Anthony* v. *Halstead* (1877) the court had to decide the contractual effect of the words 'a black horse rising five years, quiet to ride and drive and warranted sound.' It was held that the only part of the statement to constitute a warranty was 'warranted sound' and therefore the vendor had not warranted that the horse was quiet to ride and drive.

Frequently a horse is sold as 'warranted' with no further detail as to what attribute is being covered. The effect of such a statement is that the horse is being warranted as to soundness only, which means that the vendor undertakes that it has no disease or defect which actually diminishes, or in its ordinary progress will diminish, its natural usefulness. Emphysema, dropsy, navicular disease, spavin and wind galls are all examples of unsoundness, and the list could be extended twentyfold. Even slight defects, and defects which clear themselves, are breaches of the warranty, although in these cases the triviality of the purchaser's claim will be reflected in the amount of damages awarded.

The other common subject of the warranty is freedom from vice. The case of *Scholefield* v. *Robb* (1839) decided that vice means either a defect in temper which makes the horse dangerous or diminishes its usefulness, or a bad habit which is injurious to its health. Here again examples are legion, including crib-biting, kicking, rearing, weaving and wind-sucking; in fact the list is so extensive that a horse which is warranted sound and free from vice could almost be said to be the perfect animal.

Soundness and freedom from vice are not the only attributes capable of warranty. The possibilities are endless and extend to every quality which a purchaser may be looking for and which a vendor is prepared to offer. As already seen a warranty has been given to the effect that a horse had been hunted with the Bicester and, in the *Anthony* v. *Halstead* case, there would have been nothing to prevent a warranty that the horse was quiet to ride and drive, if the correct words had been used. In addition other cases have dealt with warranties that a mare has been served by a particular stallion and that another was quiet to shoe and box. No doubt other forms of wording will come before the courts but, so long as the clause in question represents an undertaking by the vendor, no matter what the subject matter, the wording will generally be construed as a warranty.

Sale of Goods Acts

Up to now we have dealt with cases where the vendor is prepared to give an express warranty, but, if he is not, are there any terms implied into the contract to cover the gap? The answer is that the Sale of Goods Act 1893, as amended by the Supply of Goods (Implied Terms) Act 1973, implies several conditions of which the most important, for the purposes of this chapter, are those contained in section 14 of the 1893 Act amended by section 3 of the 1973 Act. As they are of considerable relevance to the buying and selling of horses they are quoted verbatim below:

'14(2) Where the seller sells goods in the course of a business, there is an implied condition that the goods supplied under the contract are of merchantable quality, except that there is no such condition:

(a) as regards defects specifically drawn to the buyer's attention before the contract is made; or

(b) if the buyer examines the goods before the contract is made, as regards defects which the examination ought to reveal.

(3) Where the seller sells goods in the course of a business and the buyer, expressly or by implication, makes known to the seller any particular purpose for which the goods are bought, there is an implied condition that the goods supplied under the contract are reasonably fit for that purpose, whether or not that is a purpose for which such goods are commonly supplied, except where the circumstances show that the buyer does not rely, or that it is unreasonable for him to rely, on the seller's skill and judgement.'

The first thing to be noted in connection with both paragraphs is that the sale must be in the course of a business. The terms are not implied into a sale between private persons, who must expressly include their wording if they wish them to be incorporated. The business does not need to be a horse-dealing business, however, so that if a brewery sells its dray horses the implied terms will apply, even though the brewery is not in business for the purpose of selling horses. Horses are, of course, goods within the meaning of the Act.

For goods to be of merchantable quality within the terms of section 14(2), they must be 'as fit for the purpose or purposes for which goods of that kind are commonly bought as it is reasonable to expect, having regard to any description applied to them, the price (if relevant) and all other relevant circumstances.' It has been suggested that the term 'merchantable' can only mean commercially saleable, so if a horse is sold as an aged hack at a low price it is merchantable if it could be resold by the same description at a similar price.

Paragraph (3) is probably more generally important than paragraph (2). It would, for instance, cover the case of a father informing a dealer that he wanted a child's riding pony and the dealer selling him an unmanageable animal. The father would be able to repudiate the contract on the grounds of breach of the implied condition, and this would be so even if the father, against the dealer's advice, insisted on taking a pony which the dealer knew was unsuitable. To protect himself in the case of an unsuitable sale, the dealer would be well advised to insist that the father signed a waiver admitting that he was not relying on the dealer's skill and judgement in making the purchase. As the presumption contained in section 14(3) is in favour of such reliance, the waiver could come in useful as a means of rebuttal.

Exclusion Clauses

The vendor's right to bar out the implied conditions by means of an exclusion clause is severely limited by the 1973 Act. In the case of a consumer sale any exclusion clause seeking to exempt the vendor from the consequences of a breach of the implied conditions contained in section 14 is void. In the case of any other type of sale it is void unless it satisfies the requirement of reasonableness contained in section 55(5) of the 1893 Act, as amended. A sale is a consumer sale when made by a seller in the course of his business of goods ordinarily bought for private use or consumption and sold to a person who does not buy or hold himself out to buy in the course of a business. A sale of horses between horse dealers does not, therefore, constitute a consumer sale, but a sale of a horse by a horse dealer to a private individual, does. Sales by auction are expressly excluded from the definition, so auction particulars can contain a valid clause indemnifying the vendor against the consequences of section 14, but only if the clause meets the test of reasonableness.

The question of what is a reasonable exclusion clause is one to be answered by the courts, but guidelines are given in section 55(5). For instance, the strength of the bargaining positions of the seller and the buyer must be considered, with particular attention to the availability of suitable alternative products. Also the question of whether the buyer knew, or ought reasonably to have known, of the existence of the clause is relevant. As the test of reasonableness will only be used, in the context of horse sales, in dealings between private individuals (business transactions being excluded as 'consumer sales'), it is likely that the conditions will be easily satisfied, but more case law is required before any firm conclusions can be drawn.

It should be noted that section 14 implies conditions, and not warranties, into the contract. These conditions will, however, be converted into warranties if, between the sale and the return of the horse, the purchaser does something with it inconsistent with the seller's ownership. The buyer has to be given a reasonable opportunity of examining his purchase, but if thereafter he acts in a way which indicates he has accepted ownership, he cannot repudiate the contract. A case might be if the buyer bought the horse, examined it, found a breach of the implied condition and then put it up for sale, only returning it after he found he was unable to sell. He would not, in such circumstances, be able to rely on the remedies for breach of condition, as his attempted sale was an act of ownership, but his right to claim damages for breach of warranty would not be lost.

Trade Description Acts

Claims for damages and for rescission of the contract are civil matters, but the sale of a horse can also give rise to a criminal charge under the Trade Description Acts 1968-1972. Under this legislation a person is guilty of an offence if, in the course of a trade or business, he supplies or offers to supply any goods to which a false trade description is applied. The Acts define trade descriptions and particular reference is made to animals. To wrongly describe a horse's sex, breeding, fertility or soundness are all offences, although the seller has a defence if he can show he relied on information supplied to him or had taken all reasonable precautions to avoid the misleading description. Once again it should be noted that the offence arises out of a sale in the course of a trade or business so it does not apply to a private transaction.

Misrepresentation

Although offences under the Trade Description Acts are criminal in nature and so do not, of themselves, give the purchaser a right to claim damages, the same facts which give rise to a prosecution could also form the basis of a civil claim. To describe a racehorse in a sales catalogue as 'by Blakeney', when its sire was an indifferent hurdler can have two effects. In the first instance it can lead to a prosecution under the Acts and, in the second, it can entitle the purchaser to either rescind the contract or claim damages for misrepresentation. Warranties and conditions have been considered and seen to be actual terms of the contract. A misrepresentation, on the other hand, is a statement of fact, made by one party to the other, with the intention of inducing that party to enter into the contract, and which does have that result. It is outside the contract, but nonetheless affects the contract by giving the misled party the right to terminate it or claim damages.

Veterinary Certificates

Apart from the terms implied by the Sale of Goods Acts, the purchaser's protection up to now is seen to be based on the fact that the vendor has been prepared to speak up. Faced with a silent vendor the purchaser is back in the jungle of *caveat emptor*. It is no offence for a seller to fail to reveal a defect, it only becomes an offence when he makes a misleading statement or gives a condition or warranty which is subsequently broken. In the case of a purchase from a horse dealer his silence may not have too unacceptable an effect on the purchaser's remedies, because of the implied terms, but in a private transaction the buyer has only one weapon left in his armoury – to call in his vet for a certificate. If tempted to question the cost of this certificate the purchaser would do well to bear in mind that he is, in effect, buying a limited form of guarantee. In giving the certificate the vet is putting his professional skill on trial as, if he should make a mistake, he lays himself open to a claim based on negligence.

Few, if any, vets will nowadays give a warranty as to soundness. The reason for this is only too obvious from a cursory glance at the definition and at the obscure, and sometimes minor, defects which have been held to constitute unsoundness. The normal form of certificate is to the effect that the vet has examined the horse in accordance with a standard form of practice laid down by the joint veterinary bodies and has found no clinical signs of disease, injury or physical abnormality which would be likely to affect its usefulness for the purpose for which the purchaser has informed him he is buying it. In giving the certificate the vet must exercise the standard of skill normally possessed by persons in his profession, which means that he is not required to be a genius, but if he misses something which a normally careful vet would have spotted, then he can be sued for negligence.

Sometimes the vendor will obtain a certificate of veterinary examination and offer it with the horse. This practice is far from ideal as, with the best will in the world, it leaves the vet serving two masters. Despite the fact that the vet's contractual client is the vendor, the purchaser could have a claim against him for negligence, in addition to any claim he may have against the vendor for misrepresentation. It used to be thought that only a contractual client could sue his professional adviser for negligence, but the case of *Hedley Byrne & Co Ltd* v. *Heller & Partners Ltd* (1964) has opened up the avenue for actions by third parties. The case decided that a person who exercises a skilled profession is liable for failure to use the proper degree of care, even in the absence of contractual relationship, if the person to whom his careless advice is given is relying on him, provided that the reliance is reasonable and the adviser knows, or ought to know, that his statement is being relied on. A vet who gives a certificate to a vendor to help in a sale must know that the purchaser will be relying on that certificate, so he can hardly complain if he is sued under the Hedley Byrne case. Not only must the buyer beware, therefore, but so also should the veterinary practitioner.

Chapter 5

WHERE TO RIDE

As more and more open land disappears under bricks and concrete, and as even the quietest of country lanes is now carrying more traffic than ever before, the identification and preservation of bridleways must be an important objective of every rider. The British Horse Society recognises this and has on more than one occasion shown its teeth to good effect. If for no other reason membership of the Society is money well spent, especially as ever-spiralling costs make such important cases as *R.* v. *Secretary of State for the Environment ex parte Hood* (1975) increasingly expensive to fight. This case, taken by the B.H.S. to the Court of Appeal, will be outlined later in the chapter, but some background is necessary in order to understand it.

DEFINITIVE MAPS

Under the National Parks and Access to the Countryside Act of 1949 County Councils were given the duty to survey their areas to identify alleged public rights of way. Following the survey came a complicated procedure, involving the publication of draft maps, provisional maps and ultimately definitive maps, which had the effect of making certain facts conclusive. To quote from section 32: 'Where the map shows a bridleway, or a road used as a public path, the map shall be conclusive evidence that there was at the said date a highway as shown on the map, and that the public had thereover at that date a right of way on foot and a right of way on horseback or leading a horse so, however, that this paragraph shall be without prejudice to any question whether the public had at that date any right of way other than the rights aforesaid.'

If, therefore, the local definitive map shows a bridleway, a bridleway exists and cannot be questioned and, if it shows a road used as a public path, again it can be used by riders without query. It was the status of this latter type of highway which formed the subject of the British Horse Society's case. The 1949 Act defined a road used as a public path as being a highway, other than a public path, used by the public mainly for the purposes for which footpaths or bridleways are so used. In other words it is something more than a footpath or a bridleway, but it includes both, a typical example being the Icknield Way over the Berkshire Downs. The Act provided for periodical reviews of the definitive map at which rights of way could be upgraded as, say, from footpath to bridleway, but could not be downgraded. The Countryside Act 1968 created a slightly different kind of review, called 'a special review', one of the reasons for which was to do away with the expression 'a road used as a public path'. In future such rights of way had to be re-classified into either byways open to all traffic, or bridleways, or footpaths. The Kent County Council tried to use the special review to downgrade a road used as a public path into a footpath only. In doing this they were trying to over-ride the conclusiveness of section 32 of the 1949 Act by abolishing the bridleway aspect of this particular right of way, so the B.H.S. took up the case and, after losing in the High Court, established in the Court of Appeal that even the special review is not able to diminish the public's right to ride once that right has been included in a definitive map. It was accepted that, by virtue of express provisions in the Act, the special review could remove the right for vehicular traffic to use a road used as a public path but, in the absence of similar express provisions relating to walkers and riders, their rights could not be abolished.

When planning a ride across country the first step is to consult the definitive map. If a bridleway is marked, well and good, but what is the position if a path is marked as a footpath when the rider knows full well that it has always been used as a bridlepath? Unfortunately, in *Suffolk County Council* v. *Moon* (1978), the Court of Appeal have decided that in such a case the path can only be used as a footpath, despite its previous history. Section 32(4)(a) of the 1949 Act provides that the definitive map is conclusive, therefore if it shows a path as a footpath, then a footpath it is. Later in the chapter it will be seen that there are provisions for reviewing the map, at which time the designation may be altered if the evidence is strong enough, but until the review takes place the public's rights are limited to those shown in the map.

CREATION OF BRIDLEWAYS

It may be useful at this stage to consider how bridleways are created. By common law a bridleway, or indeed any other public highway, comes into existence when a person, who is legally competent to do so, dedicates to the public part of his land for the purpose of passage. In addition the public must have accepted such dedication, but this is generally inferred from the fact they have used it. No formal act of dedication is required, it is sufficient that the land owner has allowed use without interference for a length of time justifying an inference of dedication. How long this time needs to be formerly created problems, but the Highways Act 1949 provides that open and uninterrupted user for a period of twenty years or more is sufficient, bearing in mind that it is open to the land owner to rebutt the presumption if there are circumstances to show that the user has not amounted to full dedication.

Whether a path is a footpath or a bridleway depends upon the terms of the dedication. If a land owner allows walkers, but not riders, to cross his land, he is dedicating a footpath. If he allows both, the path will be a bridleway, usable by walkers, riders and, because of the provisions of the Countryside Act 1968, pedal cyclists. By virtue of the Act the latter will be allowed to use the bridleway even if the land owner had no such intention when he made the dedication. As well as specifying the type of use for the pathway, the land owner can also impose conditions. He can, for example, dedicate a footpath subject to his right to plough it at certain seasons of the year, or he may dedicate it subject to permanent obstructions, such as an unbridged stream. In such a case the rider cannot demand a bridge, even if the stream habitually becomes impassable in times of flood.

Most bridleways used by riders in modern times will have found their way on to the map under their correct description, but it is still possible to unearth evidence to show that a right of way, now used only as a footpath, was originally dedicated as a bridlway. If such evidence is to hand the bridleway must still be in existence, despite the fact it has fallen into disuse. The old saying, 'once a highway always a highway', reflects the fact that the public cannot give up rights once they have been acquired. They may lose their rights by stopping-up orders, or similar statutory measures, but they cannot lose them merely by non-use. In providing for reviews of the definitive map under the 1949 Act, Parliament foresaw that old rights might be overlooked for, by section 33, the highway authority is enabled to revise the map if it discovers new evidence of such a nature that, if it was then preparing the draft map, it would be required to show on the map, as a highway of a particular description, a way not so shown on the definitive map. Unfortunately the standards observed by County Councils and their successors in preparing the maps and conducting the reviews has varied enormously throughout the country. Some Authorities have prepared well-researched maps which are kept up to date, whilst others have maps which were hastily flung together and are not regularly and properly reviewed.

LIMITATION ON USE OF BRIDLEWAYS

When using a bridleway it is essential to remember that it is dedicated to the public for the purpose of passage only. The term 'passage' has been extended to include actions not strictly within the literal definition, such as resting, and even stopping, say, to sketch for a reasonable length of time, but the courts will draw the line somewhere. In *Hickman* v. *Maisey* (1900) a length of public highway ran across a stretch of land which Hickman rented out to a racehorse trainer for gallops. Maisey was a racing tipster who found that from one section of road, approximately fifteen yards long, he could watch the gallops, so gaining valuable information for his business. Hickman sued Maisey for trespassing on the road, and won. When a man dedicates a highway he retains the land over which it runs so, if any member of the public misuses the highway by stepping outside the purposes for which the land was dedicated, the land owner retains his residual common-law remedies (such as the action for trespass) which can be used against the offender. In this case it was held that, although the road was a public highway, and although Maisey had not remained stationary, but had paced up and down the fifteen-yard stretch for about one-and-a-half hours, his use of the road exceeded the ordinary and reasonable use of a highway for travel and had so infringed Hickman's rights.

Under the above principle it is likely that a similar decision would be reached, resulting in damages for trespass, if a rider allowed his horse to graze on a bridleway or even on a roadside verge. The authority for this is *Stevens* v. *Whistler* (1809) which related to cows, but could equally apply to horses as well. The same principle would also prevent a rider using a bridleway as a private gallop by passing up and down it time and time again, with no intention of using it for its proper purpose of providing a means of travelling from A to B.

STATUTORY BRIDLEWAYS

Ancient bridleways were created by dedication, but nowadays statute has taken a hand. Under the provisions of the Highways Act 1959, where it appears to a local authority that there is need for a footpath or a bridleway over land in their area and they are satisfied that it is expedient that one should be created, they may make an order, called a public path creation order. If and when the order is confirmed by the Secretary of State the footpath or bridleway comes into existence and is included in the next review of the definitive map. Pressure from riders could, therefore, have the effect of persuading the council to create a totally new bridleway, but it could also have the effect of persuading them to improve an existing one by using the same powers to take in more land to widen it.

OBSTRUCTIONS

Sometimes a rider will find that a bridleway has been obstructed as, for instance, by a locked gate or a newly erected fence. Such obstructions are generally, but not invariably, illegal both at common law, as a nuisance, and under statute, as a breach of the Highways Act 1959. Certain forms of obstruction may, however, be permissible, so two checks should be made before registering a complaint. Firstly the statement attached to the definitive map should be consulted. A pathway can, as already seen, be dedicated subject to a condition and, if this had been the case, such condition should be noted in the statement. It is conceivable that a land owner might have dedicated the way subject to the right to put a gate across it, with the result that if he exercises that right the public can have no complaint. The second check is with the highway authority to see if the land owner has applied for permission to erect a gate. The authority have power to grant such permission if the bridleway runs across agricultural land and a gate is necessary for the efficient farming of the land. The springing up of a gated obstruction on what was once a long, open stretch of good riding country does not necessarily, therefore, create an actionable offence, although the chances are that it will.

BRIDLEWAY SIGNPOSTS

So much for physical obstructions, but there is a form of obstruction which can, for want of a better word, be described as a moral obstruction. A land owner who dislikes horses crossing his fields may be tempted to put up notices denying the existence of a bridlepath or attempting to impose stringent restrictions. If he does so, he does it at his peril for, under the provisions of the National Parks and Access to the Countryside Act 1949, any such notice erected near to a path shown on the definitive map as a public footpath or bridleway is illegal if it contains any false or misleading information likely to deter the public from using it.

Whilst dealing with signs, the Countryside Act 1968 enables a highway authority, after consultation with the owner or occupier of land, to erect signposts along a footpath or bridleway. This section is permissive, but the authority also has a mandatory duty to erect a signpost wherever a path or way leaves a metalled road. Highway authorities have, in general, observed this latter duty, but one further duty is not so well observed. By section 27(4) they have the obligation to erect such signposts as may be required along the course of a path to assist persons unfamiliar with the locality to follow its course. Section 27(4) is also mandatory but, as the question of what signs are necessary for this purpose is largely a matter of opinion, in these days of economic pressure the obligation has been widely neglected. Riding clubs and similar organisations should note, however, that any other person may erect the signs with the consent of the highway authority and the signs need not necessarily be of the conventional finger-post type. Once a signpost has been properly erected it is an offence under the Highways Act 1959 to destroy, damage or deface it.

LONG-DISTANCE BRIDLEWAYS

The National Parks and Access to the Countryside Act 1949 introduced a most interesting concept which unfortunately has borne only limited fruit so far as the rider is concerned. Where it appears to the Countryside Commission that the public should be enabled to make extensive journeys, on foot or on horseback, along a particular route, being a route which for the whole or a greater part of its length does not pass along roads mainly used by vehicles, the Commission may prepare and submit to the Secretary of State a report containing proposals and recommendations for his approval. Under this provision, after severe birth pains, several long-distance routes have been created for the walker, but only one for the rider. As the riding population increases in inverse proportion to the availability of safe places to ride, it is to be hoped that the Commission will give serious consideration to its powers under the Act and create more long-distance bridleways to complement the existing South Downs Way. To be fair, however, it is true to say that, although the South Downs Way is the only long-distance route formed completely of bridleways, other routes (notably the Ridgeway Path) include bridleways along a considerable proportion of their length.

TRESPASS

Faced with a lack of bridlepaths the rider may be tempted to trespass. The advice is, of course, don't, but as to transgress is sometimes unavoidable, a brief summary of the law might be useful. Trespass is defined as unlawful entry by one person on land in the possession of another, but it is also possible to trespass without entering the other's land. For instance it has been held a trespass to fire a gun across a boundary, to encourage a dog to run onto another's land and even to allow part of one's manure heap to fall into a river so it is carried by the wind and current onto another's land. Normally, however, trespass will involve physical entry.

If the reader ever finds himself trespassing it will probably be because he is under a misapprehension, but this is no excuse. As an example, if he is following one of the badly signposted bridleways referred to earlier and takes a wrong turning, once he leaves the path he is trespassing and it is no defence to say it was by mistake. If the rider intends to enter the land on which he is found, then he is trespassing, whether or not he knows his entry is wrongful. The word intention is important because if he enters the land involuntarily and without negligence, he can plead that as a defence. A rider who is thrown over a neighbour's fence by his normally quiet and well-behaved horse is not guilty of trespass, nor is one whose horse is startled and bolts onto a neighbour's land. In both cases the rider has crossed the boundary against his will and trespass requires a voluntary act. Whilst dealing with defences, there is authority for saying that if a land owner actively obstructs a public bridleway the public may deviate onto his adjoining land to avoid the obstruction.

Trespass whilst on the highway has given rise to a fascinating series of cases. *Hickman* v. *Maisey* has already been considered, but what of the question of riding on the grass verge? The law is not altogether clear on the point, although the case of *Steel* v. *Prickett* (1819) gives some authority for the proposition that the public's right of passage is not confined solely to the metalled surface. The reasoning behind the decision dates from a time before Mr Macadam, when strips of land on the side of the road were necessary for making a detour when the surface of the highway proper became impassable. Whether or not this is still correct, the modern answer to the question posed above depends upon what has actually been dedicated. If the carriageway and the grass verge were dedicated for public passage, the public can use them both, but if only the metalled road had been the subject of the dedication, the use of the verge constitutes a trespass. Some assistance in determining the extent of the dedication is given by the case of *A.G.* v. *Beynon* (1969) which decided that when a road runs between fences there is a presumption that the whole area between the fences is included in the highway. The presumption is rebuttable, however, and if the owner of the soil of the road can show that the fences were erected other than for the purpose of delimiting the highway, he has grounds for claiming that the metalled surface constitutes its full extent. In the face of this, any member of the public using any other part of the land between the fences would be committing trespass and this would prevent a rider from using the roadside verge. It should also be noted that it is never permissible to ride a horse on the footpath at the side of the road, as this constitutes a criminal offence.

Where an unmetalled bridleway or footpath crossing open land becomes impassable there are circumstances under which it may be possible to deviate on to adjoining land without committing a trespass. The circumstances do not arise automatically, but only when the right has been acquired by long uninterrupted user. In the same way as a public bridlepath can be dedicated, so also can a right to deviate and this right continues even if the adjoining owner subsequently fences the path off from his land. The situation can arise, therefore, in which a member of the public may leave the course of a bridlepath, cross over the fence separating it from the adjoining land and ride across the adjoining land to avoid some obstacle on the path. The right must be exercised with great circumspection and only exists when the right of way is truly impassable and when the right of deviation had existed before the fence was erected.

The occupier of land has two remedies against trespassers. He can invoke the principle of self-help or he can sue for damages combined, in the appropriate case, with a request for an injunction. Self-help consists of physically ejecting the trespasser, but only after he has been asked to leave peaceably, and even after that no more force must be used than is reasonably necessary. Ejection without the request, or using excessive force, amounts to an assault for which the tables can be turned and the occupier can be sued by the trespasser. Damages can be obtained even if the occupier has suffered no loss and the courts have the power to increase the amount of normal damages to reflect any aggravation caused by the offender's conduct. If a trespassing rider is asked to leave and he does so politely and with an apology, he may still be sued, but the damages would be small. If he refused to leave or became abusive, the damages would be loaded accordingly. If the trespass is a continuing one, or if the trespasser threatens to repeat his offence, the court can grant an injunction ordering its discontinuance.

TRESPASS AND THE HUNT

Members of a hunt have no immunity from the law of trespass. This has long been established by the leading case of *Paul* v. *Summerhayes* (1878), which also illustrates the occupier's right to use force to prevent the continuance of a trespass. The fact that more claims for trespass do not arise can only be put down, in the words of Lord Coleridge in the Summerhayes' judgement, to the fact 'that those who pursue the sport do so in a reasonable spirit, and only upon the lands of those whose consent is expressly, or may be assumed to be tacitly, given.' It used to be thought that the killing of foxes as vermin gave the hunt a right, even a duty, to pursue them wherever they ran, but Lord Coleridge pointed out that even if that right ever had existed, the main purpose of the hunt had become the sport and not the kill. Persons engaging in a sport, therefore, must do so subject to the ordinary rights of property. The case of *Baker* v. *Berkeley* (1827) had earlier established that a Master of Hounds is liable for trespass committed by members of his hunt, unless he distinctly warns them not to enter the land in question.

Chapter 6

THE HORSE ON THE ROAD

The rider's use of the highway is subject to two legal disciplines. On the one hand is the criminal law, imposed by the state to protect the individual as a member of the general public and, on the other, is the civil law. The difference between the two often causes confusion. If a driver drives recklessly, injuring a horseman in the process and ending up before a magistrates' court charged with dangerous driving, his victim sometimes finds it difficult to understand why a conviction by the magistrates does not automatically lead to an order compensating him for his injuries. The answer lies in the fact that the magistrates are judging a crime for which a penalty is demanded by the state, whilst a claim for private damages, even though based on the same facts, must generally be pursued through the civil courts although the criminal courts do have a limited power to make 'compensation orders'.

THE HORSE RIDER AND THE CAR DRIVER COMPARED

Although the rider is not as heavily circumscribed as the driver, his presence on the road is nonetheless subject to criminal sanctions. As can be imagined many of these are of ancient origin and some appear rather surprising in the context of modern road conditions, but no attempt appears to have been made to equate the position of the rider with that of the car driver. The Road Traffic Act 1972, as amended by the Road Traffic Act 1974, studiously ignores the horseman in its main provisions, with the result that a driver can be guilty of dangerous driving under the Act, but a rider cannot; a driver can be asked to take a breath test, but a rider cannot; and many similar examples. This differing treatment can lead to anomalies, none more astonishing than the one relating to traffic directions. Under the provisions of the 1972 Act it is an offence for a driver to fail to observe a direction given by a police officer engaged in the regulation of traffic, but it is no offence for a rider to ignore the same direction. The situation could arise, therefore, of a policeman, in control of a busy road junction, holding up a line of traffic, but being ignored with impunity by a horse rider, although the rider would no doubt be prosecuted under one of the provisions of the Highway Act 1835, considered below, if his action led to an accident. The rider's immunity from prosecution under this section of the Road Traffic Act is even more surprising when it is seen that the Act was expressly extended to include pedestrians.

Despite the fact that the 1972 and 1974 Acts fail to cover many actions of the rider there are other Acts, usually dating from the nineteenth century, which govern the rider's conduct on roughly similar lines. The Licensing Act 1872 is a case in point which makes it an offence for a person to be drunk while in charge, on any highway or public place, of any carriage or horse. This can be compared with section 5 of the Road Traffic Act 1972 which penalises any person who, when driving or attempting to drive a motor vehicle on a road or other public place, is unfit to drive through drink or drugs. The comparison will show a significant difference because the horseman has to be drunk to be convicted, but the motor vehicle driver has only to be unfit to drive, which requires only that his ability is impaired for the time being. Within the limitations imposed by having to strictly prove the impairment, a very little amount of alcohol will suffice to convict a driver, certainly less than would be necessary to make him drunk.

The Road Traffic Acts have slightly more relevance for the coaching enthusiast than for the rider, although he too is not bound by all of their provisions. Certain sections expressly relate to a type of vehicle defined as one drawn or propelled by animal or mechanical power, but these sections are mainly concerned with technical matters, such as the number of lights required and the power of the Secretary of State to make regulations governing brakes. The Acts do not apply to the coachman's standard of driving, so he cannot be convicted of dangerous or careless driving, although, as in the case of the rider, there are other earlier Acts which have a similar effect.

THE HIGHWAY ACT 1835

Both for the rider and the coachman the Highway Act of 1835 is the most important of these earlier enactments, so it is proposed to list its main provisions, with comments where appropriate. Once again the warning is given that the list does not follow the wording of the Act and for that reason should not be relied on for anything but general background. Reference to the Act itself is advisable when considering any specific problem.

(a) By section 72 it is an offence to wilfully ride upon any footpath by the side of the road made or set apart for the use of foot passengers. In this connection 'wilfully' does not have the overtones of perversity which might be implied from its modern meaning, but merely indicates purposely. It is also an offence to lead or drive a horse or drive a carriage on the footpath and to tether a horse in such a way that it is suffered or permitted to be on the footpath.

(b) By section 77 it is an offence for a person to act as a driver of more than two carts, but one person may act as driver of two carts provided that such carts are not drawn by more than one horse each and the horse of the rear cart is attached by a rein not exceeding four feet in length to the back of the leading cart.

(c) By section 78 it is an offence if the driver of a carriage shall ride on it, or on any horse or horses drawing it, without having some other person on foot or on horseback to guide the same. This section does not apply to a carriage driven by reins and conducted by some person holding the reins of all the horses drawing it.

(d) By the same section 78 it is an offence for the driver of a carriage on the highway to cause, by negligence or wilful misbehaviour, hurt or damage to any person, horse or goods conveyed in any carriage passing or being on the highway. This is the rough equivalent of the 1972 Act's careless driving, but it is interesting to note that section 78 does not make it an offence to cause damage to another carriage.

(e) The imagination should be controlled for this next offence created by section 78. It is an offence for the driver of a carriage to quit the carriage and go on the other side of the hedge or fence enclosing the highway. The remainder of the section clearly indicates that the purpose of this prohibition is to ensure that the driver keeps near enough to his carriage to be able to control it, but on first reading other, more earthy, reasons are suggested.

(f) It is an offence, again created by section 78, for the driver of any carriage or of any horses, mules or other beasts of burden, meeting any other carriage, horses, mules or other beasts of burden, not to keep his charges on the left or near side of the road. This does not mean that he should necessarily drive on the left of a clear road, but only that he should do so when meeting other road users.

(g) Section 78 also provides that if any person riding any horse or driving any sort of carriage shall ride or drive the same furiously so as to endanger the life or limb of any passenger, he shall be guilty of an offence. Obviously the reference to passenger is not to a passenger in a vehicle, otherwise the section would not affect a rider, but it means a passenger on the highway. Moreover *Chatterton* v. *Parker* (1914) decided that neglecting to restrain a horse may amount to dangerous driving, and danger includes not only what did occur, but what might have occurred. The case concerned the driver of a horse and trap who fell asleep whilst passing through a village. The horse took hold of its bit and bolted, so that a police constable in the village street might have been injured. The constable was not injured; the driver was only driving to the extent that he was failing to control his horse and there was no one in the trap with the driver, yet nonetheless he was found guilty under the section.

Perhaps further comment is required on paragraph (f),

which puts into statutory form the ancient saying: 'the rule of the road is a paradox quite; for if you go right you go wrong, and if you go left you go right.' As already mentioned, the rule applies only to vehicles or riders passing each other, it does not relate to driving or riding on an unoccupied road. It is no offence to ride a horse on the right-hand side of the road, but it becomes an offence to do so when meeting another rider or vehicle if the horse's position in the road causes an obstruction. The gist of the offence is obstructing free passage, so in *Nuttall* v. *Pickering* (1913) it was held that there was no breach of the Act by a waggon driver who kept to the offside of the road and signalled the driver of the only other vehicle present to overtake him on the near side. The other driver accepted his signal and, as there was ample room to execute the manoeuvre, there was no obstruction, therefore no offence. The section applies to horse riders as well as to drivers, but, by custom, a horse without a rider which is being led, or a horse led by the rider of another horse, keeps to the right-hand side of the road.

COMMON LAW NUISANCES

As well as imposing sanctions on the rider and carriage driver the 1835 Act also provides them with some protection. The all-embracing section 78 makes it an offence for any person, by negligence or misbehaviour, to prevent, hinder or interrupt the free passage of any person, carriage, horses, mules or other beasts of burden, on any highway. This provision is complemented by a fascinating bye-way of common law, outside the provisions of the Highway Act, consisting of the offence of committing a common law nuisance. There are many common law nuisances affecting the use of the highway, but the one in question dates largely from nineteenth-century decisions and is two-pronged in effect. It is comprised of either using on a highway a vehicle or engine calculated to frighten horses, or of leaving a vehicle or implement calculated to frighten horses standing on the highway or verge. By its very nature the offence is hardly likely to figure prominently in modern law reports, although it still appears to be capable of prosecution.

Traction engines emitting steam and sparks have fallen foul of the first prong of the offence and it was even suggested by Collins J. in 1894 that 'if a person has his carriage constructed and painted in such a manner as to be very conspicuous indeed, it may then become a nuisance.' The second prong counts a steam plough amongst its victims in the case of *Harris* v. *Mobbs* (1878), so it can readily be appreciated that a literal application of the law could cause complete confusion in the changed circumstances of twentieth-century highway use. Even in 1889 loopholes were beginning to appear when *Galer* v. *Robinson* queried whether the vehicle in question was calculated to frighten horses of ordinary nerve and courage, and it is more than likely that the courts would nowadays expect the horse to face with equanimity vehicles, engines and implements which would have reduced his forebears to nervous wrecks. In the face of the monstrosities appearing from time to time on the roads it would be fascinating to find out how far the courts would be prepared to go in convicting under this offence, although the experiment would probably have to be conducted out of the rider's own pocket as the Attorney General, who is responsible for conducting prosecutions of this nature, is hardly likely to proceed of his own volition.

THE HIGHWAY CODE

To return to more mundane matters, certain sections of the Highway Code refer to horses and those sections have been amplified in a supplement prepared by The Royal Society for the Prevention of Accidents in co-operation with the British Horse Society. By kind permission of ROSPA the supplement is included in the Appendix. When considering the Highway Code it should be remembered that, despite the fact that it is statutory in origin, a breach of it is not, of itself, an offence. The Code's legal standing is explained in paragraph (5) of section 37 of the Road Traffic Act 1972: 'A failure on the part of a person to observe a provision of the Highway Code shall not of itself render that person liable to criminal proceedings of any kind, but any such failure may in any proceedings (whether civil or criminal, and including proceedings for an offence under this Act, the Road Traffic Act 1960 or the Road Traffic Regulation Act 1967) be relied upon by any party to the proceedings as tending to establish or to negative any liability which is in question in those proceedings.'

Because the horse rider is not faced with the welter of criminal proceedings likely to be encountered by the car driver, section 37 and the Highway Code have more relevance for him in civil, rather than in criminal, matters. Put briefly, if a rider is sued by another road user for damages arising out of the rider's negligence the question of whether he, or the other road user, did or did not observe the Code could be a factor in deciding whether the rider had been negligent, or whether the other road user had been guilty of contributory negligence. The answer to the question is not decisive to the point at issue, but, in view of section 37, it will carry considerable weight.

CIVIL LIABILITY OF THE RIDER

Negligence

The first paragraph of this chapter referred to two legal disciplines governing the rider's use of the highway. The criminal one has been discussed and the civil one must now be considered. It has been seen that the criminal offence is pursued by the state for the protection of the public at large but, in addition, the rider may be guilty of some action, perhaps even a criminal action, which harms an individual and gives that individual a right to compensation. An action to determine liability for such compensation, and to fix its amount, is a civil action, which is based on the tort of negligence in most highway cases.

The requirements for a successful negligence action have already been outlined in Chapter 1. The wrong-doer must be in the position of owing a duty of care to the injured party, his actions must be a breach of the standard of care which his duty requires him to exercise and, in addition, the damage complained of must be a foreseeable result of that breach. As the rider on the highway almost invariably owes a duty of care to other lawful road users this aspect will be taken as read and the rest of this section devoted to the standard of care and the foreseeability of the damage. Because the latter is irrelevant unless the former is breached, consideration will first be given to measuring the standard of care required.

Along with vehicle drivers and pedestrians the rider has the duty to use such care as is reasonable, which means that he has to exercise the same degree of skill and care as would be exercised by an experienced and competent rider. The law does not recognise differing degrees of skill, therefore it is no defence for a rider to claim that he is only a novice and so incapable of attaining the required standard. The harsh realities are that he should either possess the necessary competence, or stay off the road – *Nettleship* v. *Weston* (1971).

The standard is not absolute, however, in that a rider is not required to take precautions against dangers which even the experienced and competent could not have foreseen, nor is he expected to perform miracles. In *Hammack* v. *White* (1862) the defendant was trying out a newly purchased horse in Finsbury Circus – then, as now, a busy thoroughfare. For an unexplained reason the horse became restive and ran on to the pavement, killing a man. The widow's claim for damages on the grounds of negligence failed because even her own evidence showed 'that the defendant had taken well-directed efforts to control the horse, and that the horse got on the pavement in spite of, and not because of the absence of, those efforts.' The case illustrates that damages do not automatically follow injury, but that there must also be present an act of legally recognised fault. It also shows that a man who has done all that is reasonably possible to avoid an accident cannot be held responsible for any injury arising from it. It must be said, however, that it is open to question whether the very fact of trying out a horse in Finsbury Circus would not amount to negligence in the light of modern road conditions.

A series of 'unattended horse' cases helps to show what the courts expect of the rider. In *Gayler and Pope Ltd* v. *B. Davies and Son Ltd* (1924) it was decided that to leave a horse unattended in the street does not normally constitute a negligent act, but it may do so if the horse is known to be of such a character as to require careful watching lest it bolt. Knowledge of the propensities of one's horse is, therefore, relevant in deciding how much care is required, although even injury caused by a known vice does not always lead to damages; it is a question of degree and also of what precautions have been taken. In the words of Scrutton L.J. in *Cutler* v. *United Dairies* (*London*) *Ltd* (1933): 'I cannot believe that there is a horse in England which has not shied at something in the course of its life. It is, I believe, the ordinary habit of horses, being nervous animals, to shy frequently at outside things. I am startled to hear that if a horse has once shied, the owner, if he knows of it, is responsible for any damage it may do subsequently by shying.' With these words the learned judge implied that there are certain habits of the horse which will inevitably cause accidents, but subject to his words it must be true to say that a vicious act by a horse known to possess that vice is more likely to lead to a successful negligence claim than the sudden and unexplained action of a normally quiet and well-behaved animal.

If a horse is known to be dangerous in one respect it may not be negligent to fail to take precautions against another type of danger altogether which was hitherto unsuspected. The problem was fully discussed in *Aldham* v. *United Dairies* (*London*) *Ltd* (1940) in which the defendants were owners of a milk float. They knew that the pony which was used to pulling the float was restive and prone to put its feet on the pavement when left unattended, yet, despite this, their employee left it unattended and, inevitably, it acted according to character. On this occasion, however, not only did it mount the pavement, but it also 'jabbed at' a passing pedestrian, bit her in the face, dragged her down and then pawed her with its feet. The pedestrian commenced proceedings and, amongst several defences, the Dairy pleaded that, although they knew of the likelihood of the pony mounting the pavement, they could not have foreseen the additional damage it did and so could not be expected to guard against it. The court showed it did not accept this view by holding that the defendants knew of the vice, knew that the vice was likely to cause personal injury to someone and, therefore, were responsible for such personal injury, even though it was caused in a most unexpected manner.

A higher standard of care is expected in relation to injuries to children than to adults. The rider is expected to be aware of, and guard against, the fact that his horse will attract children who will not be capable of realising the dangers involved. In *Lynch* v. *Nurdin* (1841) a driver left his van with the horse attached in a street frequented by children. A boy climbed on to the van and another led the horse away, causing the first one to fall off and suffer injuries. It was held that the driver was liable as, although it was not in itself negligent to leave the van unattended, it was negligent in this case not to foresee that children would become interested in the horse and play around it. It was the nature of the street, being one often used by children for playing, that made the difference between the defendant being responsible for the accident or completely free from blame. Lynch's case was distinguished in *Donovan* v. *Union Cartage Co Ltd* (1933), in which the facts were substantially the same, except that no horse was attached to the van. A child climbed on to the van and fell off, but this time he was not entitled to damages as there was no inherent danger in a parked van which was sound, stationary and immobile. The inherent danger in Lynch's case was the attraction of the horse, which should have been obvious to the driver, but was unlikely to be appreciated by young children. Even the most well-behaved horse, because of its size and power, is a dangerous animal and, whilst adults are expected to realise this and take the necessary precautions, children cannot be expected to recognise the danger in the same way. For this reason the rider or driver must exercise special care in the presence of children, or in places where children are likely to congregate.

Normally a horseman will not be responsible for damage caused by his horse if the damage arises through the actions of a third party. If a horse, being quietly ridden along a road, were struck by a stone thrown up by a passing car causing it to kick out and injure someone on the pavement, the injured party would not have a claim against the rider. There is an exception, however, if the intervention could have been foreseen and this exception is illustrated by *Haynes* v. *Harwood* (1935), another 'unattended horse' case. A horse and cart had been left in a street in which mischievous children were known to play. A child threw a stone at the horse, causing it to bolt and injure a policeman who successfully sued the driver for damages, his success coming despite the fact that the cause of the bolting was the action of a third party. It was held that the driver, who knew the street in question, should have foreseen the incident and so should not have left his charge unattended. All these cases place a very heavy burden on the horseman, almost requiring him to have the gift of second sight, but this is rightly so in view of the damage an uncontrolled horse is capable of causing.

Negligence and the Highway Code

A failure to observe the Highway Code, the Highway Act or even well-established customs, although not of itself negligence, can provide prima facie evidence to support a civil action. It is not obligatory to ride on the left-hand side of the road, except when meeting oncoming vehicles or animals, but it is customary to do so and the Highway Code recommends it. If, therefore, an accident occurs whilst a rider is on the right-hand side of the road he will have a case to answer, especially as the judicial definition of negligence includes 'the doing of something which a prudent and reasonable man would not do' – *Blyth* v. *Birmingham Waterworks Company* (1856). A prudent and reasonable man might fly in the face of the customary rule of the road and the dictates of the Highway Code, but not very often, and then only for a very convincing reason, so the rider must have an equally convincing reason for doing likewise. This is not to say, however, that the rider's position on the road will condemn him out of hand as there is authority for the proposition that fault does not automatically attach in a riding accident to the man on the wrong side of the road – *Wayde* v. *Lady Carr* (1823) – but it does mean to say that he must have a very good explanation as to why he was there.

Because of the evidentiary significance of the Highway Code it is important to be aware of its provisions so far as they relate to the horseman. In this context the edition published in 1978 reads:

140. Before riding a horse on the roads, make sure you can control it in traffic. When riding, keep to the left. If you are leading a horse, on foot or while riding another, you should also keep to the left and keep the led animal on your left. In one-way streets, proceed only in the direction of the traffic and keep to the left. You must not ride, lead or drive a horse on a footpath or pavement by the side of the road.

141. If you are riding a horse, you should wear a hard hat.

142. If you are riding or herding animals after sunset, you should wear light-coloured or reflective clothing and carry lights which show white to the front and red to the rear.

There are many other provisions which affect the rider in common with the driver, in fact the whole of the Code should be studied, but these are the main provisions specifically relating to the horseman. If the provisions of the Highway Code and 'Riding and Roadsense', reproduced with permission in the Appendix, are observed to the letter, the rider is very unlikely to ever be on the losing end of a negligence action arising out of an accident on the road.

Contributory Negligence

Before moving on from the standard of care, contributory negligence should be mentioned. Whilst it provides no defence to an action for negligence, it can serve to reduce the damages awarded by the degree of blame attaching to the plaintiff, so, if the defendant is ninety per cent responsible for an accident and the plaintiff ten per cent, the damages the plaintiff would have obtained had he been blameless will be reduced by ten per cent. This reduction will also be applied even if the plaintiff's actions in no way contributed to the accident itself, if they contributed to the seriousness of his injuries. This is best shown in *O'Connell* v. *Jackson* (1972) where the amount of damages awarded to a totally innocent motor cyclist was cut because he was not wearing a crash helmet. The court held that his failure in this respect had contributed to the seriousness of his injuries and, therefore, he should bear part of the blame. It is probable that the same ruling would apply to a rider who was not wearing a properly reinforced riding hat, and this probability is enhanced by section 141 of the Highway Code set out above.

Foreseeable Damage

Once it is established that the proper standard of care has not been observed the next question to decide is whether the plaintiff's injuries are a foreseeable result of the breach. If they are not, they are said to be too remote and the defendant cannot be held responsible for them. The leading case on the subject is *Overseas Tankship (UK) Ltd* v. *Morts Dock & Engineering Co Ltd* (1961), otherwise known as The Wagon Mound, which has established that damages are too remote if they are not of a kind, type or class foreseeable as a result of the defendant's negligent conduct. The case of *Aldham* v. *United Dairies (London) Ltd*, which has already been considered, illustrates the problem facing the courts. It will be remembered that the defendants claimed they could not have foreseen the extensive injuries received by the plaintiff because the pony's known vice did not appear to be one likely to lead to such a result. The court held that the known vice was likely to cause physical injury of some sort, therefore the physical injuries suffered by the plaintiff could have been foreseen.

Chapter 7

THE ANIMALS ACT 1971

The last chapter dealt with liability based on negligence, but there is another kind based on the strict liability under the Animals Act 1971. So far as the Act relates to horses it deals with certain kinds of injury they may cause and also with damage arising from their straying. It does not apply to Scotland or Northern Ireland.

SECTION 2 DAMAGE

Definition

The rather involved section 2(2) provides as follows:

'Where damage is caused by an animal which does not belong to a dangerous species, a keeper of the animal is liable for the damage, except as otherwise provided by this Act, if

(a) the damage is of a kind which the animal, unless restrained, was likely to cause or which, if caused by the animal, was likely to be severe; and

(b) the likelihood of the damage or of its being severe was due to characteristics of the animal which are not normally found in animals of the same species or are not normally so found except at particular times or in particular circumstances; and

(c) those characteristics were known to that keeper or were at any time known to a person who at that time had charge of the animal as the keeper's servant or, where that keeper is the head of a household, were known to another keeper of the animal who is a member of that household and under the age of sixteen.'

Given that a horse is not a member of a dangerous species, the first problem posed by the section is that of deciding what are its normal and abnormal characteristics. Is it normal for a horse to kick another? If it is, damages cannot be awarded under the Act, but if it is abnormal then the Act will apply. It is questionable whether it is abnormal for a horse to bite another, but however much those in daily contact with them may doubt it, *Glanville* v. *Sutton & Co Ltd* (1928) suggests that such conduct, when directed towards humans, is abnormal. Is it abnormal for a horse to shy? As already seen Scrutton L.J. thought not, but does this mean that damages can never be awarded under the Act for injuries caused by a shying horse? There are many areas of doubt to be clarified, but it does appear to be certain that the Act will apply to the horse which bites or kicks a human. How much further it goes remains to be seen, although conclusions can be drawn from studying pre-1971 cases dealing with the old common law which the Animals Act has now codified.

The Act makes provision for certain normal vices to be actionable in the same way as abnormal ones. These are the vices found in animals at a particular time or in particular circumstances, such as 'a mare at seasons when she is subject to sexual excitement' – *Manton* v. *Brocklebank* (1923). Without this provision it could be argued that a mare which caused injury whilst in such a condition was only acting normally, but the provision scotches this defence. The result is that the keeper of a mare in season or of a mare with a foal at foot will have to take special care to ensure that she does not indulge her natural tendencies to cause harm by her over-excitement or in her desire to protect her young.

To be actionable the damage must be the likely kind of damage to be caused by the known characteristic. In *Cutler* v. *United Dairies (London) Ltd* (1933) we have already seen that 'jabbing at' and biting a passer-by was the likely kind of damage to be expected from a horse known to become restive and mount the footpath when left alone. In contrast, *Bard v. O'Connor* (1960) decided that a broken ankle suffered by the plaintiff in trying to stop a dog-fight provoked by the defendant's boxer was not the likely kind of injury to be expected from the dog's fighting propensities. The result would have been different had he been bitten.

Finally, for an action to succeed, the abnormal characteristic must have been known to the keeper. This is a relict of the old wives' saying that every dog is allowed one bite, although the saying is based only on a half truth, as it is not necessary for a dog actually to bite someone for the owner to know that it has a propensity to do so. In *Worth* v. *Gilling* (1866) the defendant's dog was kept on a chain and the defendant knew it was fierce because, whenever anyone passed, it ran to the end of the chain and tried to bite them. When it finally achieved its object by biting the plaintiff it was held that it was not open to the defendant to use the animal's previous lack of success to plead that he was unaware of the danger. His action in chaining up the dog, combined with the dog's conduct whilst on the chain, made it obvious that he knew of the probability of such an occurrence.

Section 2(2)(c) provides that the keeper's knowledge of the vice can be implied when his servant, who has charge of the animal, knows of it. Servant, in this context, is not limited to the domestic servant, but extends to any employee, provided he has charge of the animal in that capacity. Because of this proviso it would be immaterial for a plaintiff to show that the defendant's housekeeper knew of the vicious tendencies of her employer's horse because she would be unlikely to be in charge of it. On the other hand it would be highly relevant to prove that the groom had the same knowledge. In *MacLean* v. *The Forestry Commission* (1970) the court refused to impute the knowledge of one employee, who was not in control of the defendant's horse, to the employee who was. It is the employee actually in charge of the horse who has to have the knowledge and knowledge possessed by any other employee is irrelevant. In his decision the judge commented: 'If each is to be regarded in his own way as the alter ego of the employers it seems to produce a schizophrenic legal persona, and I cannot imagine that the law leads to such a result.'

Who is 'the keeper'?

The question of who is the keeper of an animal is answered by section 6(3) as follows:

'(3) Subject to sub-section (4) of this section, a person is keeper of an animal if:
(a) he owns the animal or has it in his possession; or
(b) he is the head of a household of which a member

under the age of sixteen owns the animal or has it in his possession;

and if at any time an animal ceases to be owned by or to be in the possession of a person, any person who immediately before that time was a keeper thereof by virtue of the preceding provisions of this sub-section continues to be a keeper of the animal until another person becomes a keeper thereof by virtue of those provisions.'

Sub-section (4) is a saving provision to relieve a temporary keeper from liability in certain circumstances:

'(4) Where an animal is taken into and kept in possession for the purpose of preventing it from causing damage or of restoring it to its owner, a person is not a keeper of it by virtue only of that possession.'

The first thing to note from section 6 is that the owner of an animal can be liable for injuries caused by it even though it is not in his possession and even though he may have very little control over it. If a horse is left with a trainer and it injures someone, both the owner and the trainer could be liable, the trainer by virtue of possession – *Walker* v. *Hall* (1876) – and the owner by virtue of ownership, it mattering not that the owner has surrendered all control of the horse.

One further seeming anomaly is created by section 6 because of the reference to head of the household. No doubt the legislators meant the man of the house, but in these egalitarian days would this be accepted by the courts? Who is the head of a household when both husband and wife work, indeed who is the head of the household when the wife does not work? Because of equal rights for women it might be argued that there is no such thing and the household is run in partnership rather than under a chain of command. The House of Lords' debate on the Act foresaw the problem when it was asked who fulfilled the statutory definition in a household belonging to and run by two widowed sisters with children under the age of sixteen. Apart from this difficulty of interpretation the reason for the section is obvious. It is intended to cover the situation where a father seeks to avoid liability by claiming that a pet he bought for his young child, and which the child looks after, is neither in his ownership nor in his possession.

Defences to Section 2 Damage

There are three available defences to claims under section 2 of the Act, all of them contained in section 5 as follows:

'5(1) A person is not liable under sections 2 to 4 of this Act for any damage which is due wholly to the fault of the person suffering it.

(2) A person is not liable under section 2 of this Act for any damage suffered by a person who has voluntarily accepted the risk thereof.

(3) A person is not liable under section 2 of this Act for any damage caused by an animal kept on any premises or structure to a person trespassing there, if it is proved either:

(a) that the animal was not kept there for the protection of persons or property; or

(b) (if the animal was kept there for the protection of persons or property) that keeping it there for that purpose was not unreasonable.

There are two points arising from section 5 which require some amplification. The first one appears in sub-section (1) which requires the fault to be wholly that of the plaintiff. It is not sufficient that the plaintiff should have been partly to blame and the defendant the remaining part as, in such a case, the defence would not be available. Partial blame attributable to the plaintiff might help the defendant by giving him the opportunity to counter-claim for contributory negligence, but it effectively removes from him any possibility of using the statutory defence provided by sub-section (1). *Dowler* v. *Bravender* (1968) provides an example of the type of conduct which will give rise to a defence by holding that a man was wholly at fault where he provoked a horse to such an extent by shouting at it that it kicked him.

The second point appears in sub-section (2) which requires that the plaintiff should have voluntarily accepted the risk. The word 'voluntarily' implies that the plaintiff knew of the danger. A risk which is not appreciated cannot be voluntarily accepted and, as a result, a man who goes into the loose-box of a vicious horse, not knowing of its vice, cannot be said to have accepted the risk of injury. He knew of no risk, therefore he could not have assented to it.

The defence of 5(2) is severely curtailed in employer–employee cases because of section 6(5) which provides:

> 'Where a person employed as a servant by a keeper of an animal incurs a risk incidental to his employment, he shall not be treated as accepting it voluntarily.'

The effect of this section is harsh on the employer as it effectively prevents him from using the defence of section

5(2). This is so even in cases where the employee was engaged for the express purpose of taking the risk and knew of the dangers involved when he took up his employment. Thus if a man is employed to groom a stallion, which he and his employer both know has a tendency to bite, and is injured by the stallion biting him, he would be able to recover damages despite his pre-knowledge. Like much employment-protection law, section 6(5) probably goes further than necessary to protect the employee. The reason for the section is obvious; it would be too easy for an employer to order an unwilling employee to do a dangerous job with the implied threat of dismissal if he refused, but it should be possible to provide some middle course fair to both parties. It seems the only loophole in favour of the employer arises out of the question of whether the risk was incidental to the employment. If a man employed as a gardener enters the box of a vicious stallion, it is questionable whether his action is incidental to his employment, but if a groom does the same there is no doubt about it, even if the groom is paid additional money in recognition of the risk. In the case of the gardener the employer could plead section 5(2), but in the case of the groom he would have no such defence. It should be noted, however, that section 6(5) relates only to defences under section 5(2); it would not preclude a defence under section 5(1) if the employee were injured wholly because of his own fault.

SECTION 4 DAMAGE

Straying

Section 2 covers one form of damage caused by horses, but

damage caused by straying is covered by section 4, which reads as follows:

'4(1) Where livestock belonging to any person strays on to land in the ownership or occupation of another and:
(a) damage is done by the livestock to the land or to any property on it which is in the ownership or possession of the other person; or
(b) any expenses are reasonably incurred by that other person in keeping the livestock while it cannot be restored to the person to whom it belongs, or while it is detained in pursuance of section 7 of this Act or in ascertaining to whom it belongs;
the person to whom the livestock belongs is liable for the damage or expenses, except as otherwise provided by this Act.
(2) For the purposes of this section any livestock belongs to the person in whose possession it is.'

Section 4 gives a right of action for damage caused by a straying horse to the land itself or to any property on the land. An action could result, therefore, from the horse treading down a crop, or biting the plaintiff's horse – *Ellis* v. *Loftus Iron Co* (1874), but not from it kicking the plaintiff, although in this latter case the plaintiff may be able to proceed under section 2. Disregarding personal injuries, the other kinds of damage covered by section 4 are numerous. Two examples have been given, but in addition an action would lie if the defendant's half-bred stallion strayed and covered the plaintiff's thoroughbred mare. *Halstead* v. *Mathieson* (1919) even provides that an action would lie if the fact that a bull had strayed makes it impossible for the plaintiff to guarantee that his heifers are unserved, whether or not he can prove actual service.

There is some doubt still existing as to what constitutes straying. Prior to the Act liability was based on the fact that the animal had trespassed and in *Ellis* v. *Loftus Iron Co* (1874) it was held that one horse putting its head over a fence and biting another constituted sufficient trespass. In the words of Lord Coleridge: 'That may be a very small trespass, but it is trespass in law.' The Act substitutes the concept of straying for that of trespassing and the question of whether the two are synonymous has still to be decided, although the Law Commission, upon whose report the Act is founded, recommended that liability should continue to be based on trespass. In the majority of situations a trespassing horse will indisputably be a straying horse, but in common with many legal problems, it is the borderline case which creates the difficulties.

Defences to Section 4 Damage

The wording of section 4 indicates that defences are available to a claim for damages for straying livestock, but it also indicates that such defences are limited strictly to those mentioned in the Act. Once again section 5 is relevant as we have already seen that sub-section (1) relates to section 4 offences as well as those under section 2. If, therefore, the damage caused by the straying animal is wholly the fault of the plaintiff, he has no remedy. In connection with straying livestock, section 5(6) amplifies section 5(1) as follows:

> 'In determining whether any liability for damage under section 4 of this Act is excluded by sub-section (1) of this

section the damage shall not be treated as due to the fault of the person suffering it by reason only that he could have prevented it by fencing; but a person is not liable under that section where it is proved that the straying of the livestock on to the land would not have occurred but for a breach by any other person, being a person having an interest in the land, of a duty to fence.'

The combined effect of sections 5(1) and 5(6) leads to the following consequences:

(a) if A's horse strays through an unrepaired fence on to B's land, causing damage, and B has a duty to maintain that fence, then B cannot claim damages;
(b) given the same facts as in (a) except that B has no duty to maintain the fence, then he can claim damages, even if he could have kept the horse out by repairing the fence himself;
(c) if A's horse strays through an unrepaired fence on to land belonging to B but leased to C, causing damage to C's stock or crops, C's right of action will depend upon whether or not B had a duty to repair the fence. If he had, then C cannot recover damages, but if he had no such duty C can sue A. The duty referred to in this example is that between A and B and not any duty which C might owe to B arising out of his obligations under the lease or tenancy agreement.

Duty to Fence

Unfortunately the Act does not define 'duty to fence' so the pre-1971 common-law rules have to be considered. They show that the law has never imposed any obligation on a man to fence his land but that such an obligation may be created by formal agreement or may grow up through long user or custom. If a man has repaired a fence for forty years and upwards in circumstances which indicate that he thought he had a duty to do so, he cannot thereafter turn round and deny the obligation; his actions have created a liability binding on him and his successors in title. In *Egerton* v. *Harding* (1974) the defendant had a right to graze cattle on a stretch of common land which bordered the plaintiff's cottage. The defendant's cattle strayed into the plaintiff's garden and caused some damage whereupon the plaintiff sued, basing her claim on the defendant's liability to fence against his own stock. The case went to the Court of Appeal where it was held that by immemorial custom it was the responsibility of land owners around the common to fence against animals straying from it. By custom, therefore, an obligation had been imposed on the plaintiff and as she had failed to observe the obligation her case must fail. The defendant in Egerton's case was able to show that the plaintiff had a binding duty to fence, but if he had been unable to produce such proof he, as owner of the animals, would have been responsible for the damage they caused.

Section 5(5) creates a further defence:

> 'A person is not liable under section 4 of this Act where the livestock strayed from a highway and its presence there was a lawful use of the highway.'

The defence depends upon the initial use of the highway being lawful. If a horse strays on to the highway and from there into a field the horse owner has no defence, and similarly if the horse has been turned on to the highway to graze and then strays. In both cases the initial use of the highway was unlawful. On the other hand, if the initial use of the highway was lawful, the defendant could claim the protection of section 5(5), although it is possible that the plaintiff might still be able to proceed with an alternative claim in negligence. This is illustrated by *Gayler and Pope Ltd* v. *B. Davies & Son Ltd* (1924) in which the defendant's pony, which had been left unattended in the street, bolted through the plaintiff's shop window. The plaintiff sued both in trespass and in negligence and succeeded in the latter but not in the former. The case was decided well before the Animals Act, but even in 1924 it was established that a person with premises adjoining a highway is presumed to accept the risk of straying from the highway. As a consequence the trespass action failed because there was nothing to suggest that the defendant was using the highway unlawfully, but, in the words of McCardie J.: 'When a pony and van, wholly unattended, dash into a plaintiff's shop window adjoining a highway there is a prima facie case of negligence.' As the defendant was unable to rebutt the prima facie case he was held responsible for the damage.

STRAYING ON THE HIGHWAY

Under the Highways Act 1959 it is a criminal offence to allow horses to stray on to the highway but, until the Animals Act, there was no corresponding civil offence. The leading case on the point is *Searle* v. *Wallbank* (1947) in which the defendant's horse strayed on to the highway, injuring a cyclist who collided with it. The cyclist failed in his action for negligence as the court held that the owner of roadside land was under no duty to take care that his animals did not stray on to the roadway. He could be as careless as he liked over the maintenance of his roadside fences, but his carelessness would not lead to an action for negligence. The decision left the land owner in the privileged, albeit peculiar, position of being liable in trespass if his horse strayed on to his neighbour's land and ate his vegetables, but not liable if the same horse strayed on to the highway and caused a fatal accident. Section 8 of the Animals Act has now remedied this anomaly by providing that liability for damage caused by animals straying on the highway is based firmly on the general principles of negligence. If the land owner has taken reasonable care to ensure that his animals do not escape he has a good defence, but if he has taken no adequate precautions he will be vulnerable in any action taken by a highway user who is injured.

The roadside land owner does retain some privileges preserved to him by section 8(2) of the Act:

> 'Where damage is caused by animals straying from unfenced land to a highway a person who placed them on the land shall not be regarded as having committed a breach of the duty to take care by reason only of placing them there if:
>
> (a) the land is common land, or is land situated in an area where fencing is not customary, or is a town or village green; and
>
> (b) he had the right to place the animals on that land.'

Section 8 has an effect which should be considered carefully by the horse owner. As has been seen liability is now based on the common-law concept of negligence, but what has not been considered is the definition of a highway. It should be remembered that this extends to bridlepaths and footpaths, so, if a horse is placed in a field through which a bridlepath or footpath runs, the owner will be liable for any injury it does to a user of the path if he, the owner, has been negligent. As this type of path is often unfenced the possibility of liability could be a continuing worry, although it has been suggested in *Fitzgerald* v. *E. D. & A. D. Cooke Bourne (Farms) Ltd* (1964) that 'it would be too much to expect that an "ordinarily careful" owner of fillies should refrain from keeping them in a field where there is a public highway merely because there is a chance that one of the fillies in a playful mood might come in contact with and injure someone lawfully walking along the highway.' Each case will be decided on its merits, however, so that even if the suggestion outlined above forms the basis of a good defence it would be otherwise if the fillies were known to be dangerous and likely to attack people.

THE INJURED PARTY'S REMEDIES

As well as making a claim for damages, a person whose land or property is damaged by a straying animal has the additional remedy of detaining the stray, provided that at the time it is not under anyone's control. Following from this he has the right to sell the animal, either at a market or by public auction, after he has lawfully detained it for fourteen days. He cannot, however, both sue and sell, he must choose one remedy or the other. Whilst in his custody the animal must be treated with reasonable care and supplied with adequate food and water. The detainer must also inform a police officer of his action within 48 hours and the owner must be informed if his identity is known. The sale proceeds may be retained only to the extent required to cover the cost of keep and the damage sustained, the remainder must be paid to the animal's owner. The right of detention is created by section 7 of the Act and replaces the old remedy of distress damage feasant.

Chapter 8

THE HORSE IN SPORT

The horse lends itself naturally to providing sport at all levels, from the Pony Club gymkhana to the Epsom Derby, but, because of its speed and size, such sport can often be dangerous. It is advisable, therefore, for competitors, organisers and even spectators to be conscious of their legal duties and to make sure that they are observed. A breach of duty can lead to serious consequences in terms of damages, so should be carefully guarded against. The types of case which might give rise to an action are four in number and are examined below:

ACTIONS BETWEEN COMPETITORS

If a competitor is injured whilst pursuing his sport it is highly unlikely that he would even consider suing the person who caused the injury. This is a commonly accepted fact which the law recognises by providing that a person engaged in playing a lawful game takes on himself the risks incidental to being a player and has no remedy by action for injuries received in the course of the game. There are, however, circumstances in which this rule is inapplicable and in which an action for damages might lie. To understand those circumstances it must be appreciated that the rule is based upon the wider doctrine of *volenti non fit injuria*, meaning that the injured party freely and voluntarily, with full knowledge of the nature and extent of the risks he ran, impliedly agreed to incur them. The doctrine is not confined to actions involving injury in sport but, within certain limits, relates to any situation in which an action for negligence might lie. The essence of *volenti* is knowledge of the risk involved, so if a person enters into a dangerous situation not knowing of the danger, he cannot be said to have agreed to incur it. By virtue of his participation the sportsman is entering into a dangerous situation and the law provides that he is presumed to do so with his eyes open. His presumed knowledge, however, is only extended to the risks incidental to the game as these are the ones he has foreseen and these are the ones he has agreed to incur. If he is injured by another type of risk his right to take action remains unimpaired. Between competitors this leads to the result that there is no claim for damages for injuries caused in the normal course of the game, but if one competitor acts unfairly, or is guilty of foul play and by his conduct injures another, that other can sue.

In the above context 'unfair conduct' and 'foul play' are not necessarily synonymous with a breach of the rules of the game. A rule can be broken, causing injury, which does not give rise to a claim for damages; in fact it is very unusual for it to do so. For the offence to be actionable it must be well outside the degree of violence normally expected in the game in question. Deliberately attempting to ride an opponent over the rails in a horse race would qualify, but it is doubtful whether damages would be given in a situation where one jockey had taken the other's ground with no intention to harm and not in a reckless or dangerous manner.

ACTIONS BETWEEN COMPETITORS AND ORGANISERS

A competitor, as seen above, by participating in a game or sport accepts the incidental risks involved. In some cases the actions, or perhaps lack of action, of the organiser can introduce a completely new risk which was not contemplated by the competitor and for which, therefore, he retains his right to sue. The leading case on the subject is *Gillmore* v. *London County Council* (1938) in which the County Council organised and ran a physical training class on their premises. The plaintiff was taking part in an exercise involving physical contact with other members of the class when he lost his footing and fell on the exceptionally slippery floor, thereby injuring himself. He sued the Council which sought to rely on the defence of assumption of risk. The court ruled against the defence and upheld the plaintiff, holding that he had certainly consented to run certain risks by joining the class, but risk of injury from a slippery floor was not one of them. Such an injury was quite outside the normal incidental dangers of a physical contact sport, so could not have been in the plaintiff's contemplation when he impliedly assumed the risks of the activity.

In contrast with Gillmore's case is *Simms* v. *Leigh Rugby Football Club Ltd* (1969) in which Simms was a member of a visiting team playing at Leigh. He was fairly tackled by an opponent but unfortunately the tackle knocked him into a concrete wall slightly over seven feet from the playing area. He claimed that his collision with the wall had broken his leg, although it appears that this was never satisfactorily proved as he might have broken his leg in the tackle. In any event he sued the Club on the grounds that the wall was erected in a dangerous position and, in their defence, the Club produced the bye-laws of the Rugby League which provided that no more than a seven-foot gap was required between the pitch and the spectators' enclosure. Because of the fact that the wall complied with the bye-laws they claimed that whether or not it was erected in a safe position was immaterial because the plaintiff had not only assumed the risk inherent in the physical contact of the game, but also any risk which might flow from the implementation of the directions of the governing body. The court accepted the defence and ruled that Simms had indeed assumed the latter risk so was not entitled to succeed.

Where the organiser of a sport or game is also the occupier of the land on which it is played the Occupier's Liability Act of 1957 requires him to exercise the common duty of care towards his visitors. Persons engaged in the sport are classified as visitors so may have an action under the Act if they are injured because of the condition of the premises. If, therefore, an occupier provides a jumping arena in which there is a rabbit hole which causes a horse to trip and throw its rider, the rider could sue. Dangerous obstructions on a racecourse could give rise to a similar result, especially if they are unnecessary and have no relevance to the event.

ACTIONS BETWEEN COMPETITORS AND SPECTATORS

The leading case on this type of action is *Wooldridge* v. *Sumner and Another* (1962) which revolved around an incident at the White City National Horse Show of 1959.

Mr Sumner had entered a heavy hunter of the highest quality which was being shown for him by Ronald Holladay, himself a competitor of great skill and experience. About two feet from the edge of the ring was a line of tubs interspersed with benches and between the tubs and the spectators was a cinder track. Mr Wooldridge, a film cameraman, was standing near to one of the benches about twenty-five yards from a corner of the ring in the grandstand straight. It was shown in evidence that the hunter, named Work of Art, was a particularly impressive horse at all paces, but its best form was shown at the gallop. Because of this Mr Holladay was taking particular care to ensure that it galloped as fast as possible to impress the judges, as was his duty as a competitor. On rounding the corner and entering the grandstand straight the horse went behind the row of tubs, appearing to jump one in the process, and galloped down the wrong side towards the plaintiff. Mr Wooldridge had no experience of horses and when he saw Work of Art approaching him he took fright and stepped back or fell into its path, receiving fairly severe injuries. In the High Court the judge held that the rider had approached the corner too quickly; because of this he was negligent and so his principal, Mr Sumner, was liable in damages to the plaintiff. On appeal it was decided that Mr Holladay's riding of the horse was not negligent, his approach into the corner was not the cause of the action and any mistake he may have made amounted merely to an error of judgement, which is not in itself an actionable offence. Diplock L.J. expressed it: 'If in the course of a game or competition at a moment when he really has not time to think, a participant by mistake takes a wrong measure, he is not, in my view, to be held guilty of any negligence.'

The subsequent case of *Wilks* v. *Cheltenham Car Club*

(1971) shows that Wooldridge's case does not give the competitor carte blanche to act as recklessly as he pleases. There is a limit beyond which he must not go and this limit is explained by Edmund Davies L.J. in the later case: 'Nevertheless, although in the very nature of things the competitor is all out to win and that is exactly what the spectators expect of him, it is in my judgement still incumbent on him to exercise such degree of care as may reasonably be expected in all the circumstances. For my part, therefore, I would hold him liable only for damage caused by errors of judgement or lapse of skill going beyond such as, in the stress of circumstances, may reasonably be regarded as excusable.'

ACTIONS BETWEEN SPECTATOR AND ORGANISER

Although Wooldridge's case and Wilks' case were pursued against the competitors in the Court of Appeal, both of the plaintiffs had originally joined in the organisers in the lower court. That the organisers figured in neither appeal decision is due to the fact that their safety arrangements were satisfactory. In Wilks' case it was found that they had done all that was reasonable in that they had erected a recommended form of fencing between the track and the spectators, they had driven the stakes well in, kept the ropes taut and had observed all the requirements of the Auto-Cycle Union for events of that nature. There were similar findings in favour of the British Horse Society and the proprietors of the White City Stadium in Wooldridge's case. Nevertheless they had been at risk and organisers of sporting events should take all reasonable precautions to ensure the safety of spectators. The extent of their duty is outlined in *Hall* v. *Brooklands Auto-Racing Club* (1932): 'What is reasonable care would depend on the perils which might be reasonably expected to occur, and the extent to which the ordinary spectator might be expected to appreciate and take the risk of such perils.'

The above definition suggests that a spectator's claim for damages can be defeated by the *volenti* defence, and this is in fact the case. It must not be supposed, however, that once the spectator buys his ticket he has accepted every risk which comes his way, leaving the organiser free from any responsibility. The organiser retains certain duties and those duties are set out in the above definition. Because of the *volenti* principle, however, the duties are not excessively onerous and in no way can be taken to mean that the organiser guarantees the safety of the spectator. In *Hunt* v. *Stephens* (1963) a mother was carrying her child in her arms at a small local agricultural show. Typical of many such shows, horses were ridden in the same area as that open to the public before they were taken into the ring to compete. The mother stepped into the path of a trotting horse in the common area thereby dropping the child. She sued the organiser of the event, claiming that he was negligent for not completely fencing off the horses from the spectators or, alternatively, for not issuing adequate instructions to riders to prevent them mixing with the public. The claim failed on several counts, all of them of considerable comfort to the show secretary. It was held that organisers of shows are entitled to assume that horses brought there are well behaved and well mannered. It was also recognised that it was common practice to allow horses and spectators to mix at such events, so there was no negligence in not providing separate enclosures. Finally it was accepted that most people attending small country shows would be used to horses and therefore aware of the danger attaching to them. The court decision went in favour of the show organiser but there is a possibility that in similar circumstances an action against the rider, rather than against the organiser, might succeed.

In the majority of cases spectators attend sporting events under a contractual relationship with the organiser. Because of this the provisions of section 5(1) of the Occupier's Liability Act 1957 are relevant:

> 'Where persons enter or use, or bring or send goods to, any premises in exercise of a right conferred by contract with a person occupying or having control of the premises, the duty he owes them in respect of dangers due to the state of the premises or to things done or omitted to be done on them, in so far as the duty depends on a term to be implied in the contract by reason of its conferring that right, shall be the common duty of care.'

The nature of the common duty of care has already been examined in Chapter 1 as have also the provisions of the Unfair Contract Terms Act of 1977 in relation to attempts to avoid liability by means of exclusion clauses. There is nothing to prevent the organiser from posting up notices seeking to avoid liability for negligence, breach of contract or non-observance of the 1957 Act, but he should bear in mind that the notices are valueless so far as they seek to avoid liability for personal injury and are of only limited effect in other cases. The test of reasonableness has to be borne in mind, so that if the notices fail to meet the test, they provide no defence.

CRIMINAL LIABILITY

So far in this chapter we have concentrated on civil liability for sporting injuries, but there are, in addition, criminal implications, usually arising out of assault and battery, although in extreme cases manslaughter may have to be considered. Assault and battery are two distinct crimes usually lumped together in everyday parlance as assault. They are defined as follows: an assault is an act whereby one person intentionally causes another to apprehend immediate and unlawful personal violence; a battery is an intentional act actually inflicting such violence. It should be noted that no hostile intent is necessary, so to ride one's horse deliberately at another, even in jest, in such a way as to cause fear of personal injury is an assault. It can readily be seen, therefore, that most sports and games involve actions which might amount to assault or battery, but which very rarely do.

Take, for instance, the hunting accident in which one rider jumps a hedge, landing on top of another who has fallen. There is obviously no battery here because there is no element of intention, but what if the jump were made recklessly, with no intention to harm but careless of the consequences? A case in point might be where a following rider saw another jump a fence, disappear for a moment and then his horse appear riderless. In such circumstances it would probably be regarded as civil negligence to deliberately jump the fence in the same place, but is it a crime? The point has not yet been conclusively settled, but there is some reason for thinking that sufficiently reckless conduct can provide the 'intention' element in battery – *R.* v. *Bradshaw* (1835).

Intention in one form or another is an essential element of the crime but there are many sports free from a history of criminal prosecution in which intentional physical contact is a positive virtue. Boxing, wrestling and football are all examples as is the riding-off element in polo. Why they are free from prosecution is, of course, due to the *volenti* element which has already been considered in conjunction with civil liability. It is the essence of both assault and battery that they are done against the will of the injured party so, if it can be shown he has consented to the act complained of, no offence is committed. By participating in the sport the injured party is presumed to have given his consent, even if some of the injuries done to him are inflicted in a manner outside the rules of the game. The decision in *R.* v. *Bradshaw* suggests, however, that there is a limit to what must be endured before sporting violence becomes a crime. In his ruling Bramwell L.J. stated that if a footballer in charging 'was indifferent and reckless as to whether he would produce serious injury or not, then the act would be unlawful.' The decision is not completely decisive, however, because the word 'unlawful' could have meant either criminally unlawful or unlawful in a civil context.

Sometimes a sporting injury results in death. Whether or not this will amount to manslaughter or accidental death depends very much upon whether the incident which caused the death was an unlawful act. As has been seen, many sports, including most of those involving horses, entail the risk of physical injury as almost a prerequisite of participation. If death follows such an injury it would be classified as accidental unless there were some element of excessive violence quite outside the normal on the part of some other participant, in which case it is quite possible that a manslaughter verdict would follow. Once again it must be emphasised that violence outside the rules does not *ipso facto* amount to an unlawful act. In *R.* v. *Moore* (1898) Hawkins J. stated that a breach of the rules was not even admissible in evidence to prove an unlawful act 'for it is not criminal and not necessarily either dangerous or malicious to break them.'

NATURAL JUSTICE

To be able to participate in an equine event often necessitates joining some organisation or club having control of the sport, or obtaining from them a licence to train or ride. The act of joining or taking the licence constitutes a contract wherein it is accepted that the rules and regulations of the organisation will be observed. The courts will generally only intervene between the parties when the organisation is in breach of the contract or has not exercised its powers under the contract fairly and in good faith and in accordance with the rules of natural justice. From time to time the courts have been asked to intervene in cases where no obvious contractual relationship exists, probably the most famous being *Nagle* v. *Fielden* (1966). Mrs Nagle had made application for a licence to train racehorses and had been refused by the Jockey Club. She was convinced that the refusal was based purely and simply on the grounds that she was a woman and her conviction tended to be borne out by the fact that a licence had been granted to her head lad without demur. She applied to the court, therefore, seeking *inter alia* a declaration that it was against public policy for a refusal to be based on such grounds. The case came to the Court of Appeal, not on its merits, but on whether Mrs Nagle had even any right to make the application. In the lower court the Jockey Club had successfully sought to have the action struck out on the basis that it was wrong in law as there was no contractual relationship between Mrs Nagle and themselves, therefore the court had no power to interfere with their discretion to grant or withhold a licence. The decision in the lower court led to a situation which the Court of Appeal was not prepared to accept. It meant that unless Mrs Nagle were granted a licence there would be no contractual relationship so, if the lower court were right, there would be no opportunity for the courts to decide whether the licence had been refused capriciously. It was felt by the Appeal Court that the principle involved was too important for judicial review to be blocked in such a manner so they ordered that the case should be allowed to go to trial on its merits. Lord Denning outlined the issue at stake very forcibly: 'The common law of England has for centuries recognised that a man has a right to work at his trade or profession without being unjustly excluded from it. He is not to be shut out from it at the whim of those having the governance of it. If they make a rule which enables them to reject his application arbitrarily or capriciously, not reasonably, that rule is bad.'

The Nagle case made a dent in the general rule requiring contractual relationship as a prerequisite of judicial interference and it is now accepted that the courts may intervene when an organisation has made a decision which affects personal status or the right to work, whether or not a contract is involved. This does not mean they will interfere lightly. They will generally only be prepared to act when the organisation has a duty to act judicially and has abused that duty. Even then the matter must be one of substance, as perhaps a disciplinary decision carrying a substantial penalty.

Once the courts do become involved they will be concerned to ensure that the organisation has acted in accordance with its rules and also that it has observed the rules of natural justice. There is always a tendency for the losing party to believe that natural justice has been flouted in his case and this tendency has led to many widely differing suggestions as to what the concept actually embraces. When the decisions are considered, however, it can be seen that the definition goes no further than two main principles: that no man shall be a judge in his own cause and that no man shall be condemned unheard.

No man shall be a judge in his own cause

The first leg of the definition means that where a person has a direct interest in the subject matter of an inquiry he should disqualify himself from adjudicating on it. The obvious example arises out of the existence of a financial interest, but the rule also applies where there is likelihood of any other form of bias. It would be wrong, therefore, for the same person to act as prosecutor and judge and also for a member of the adjudicating body to act as a witness. A personal relationship with the accused could serve to disqualify as could an expression of partisanship before the hearing. The test is whether a reasonable person, acquainted with the outward appearance of the situation, would have reasonable grounds for suspecting bias. In the presence of bias the courts have the right to set the decision aside unless the complainant, with full knowledge of the facts, has expressly or impliedly waived his right to object.

No man shall be condemned unheard

The second leg requires the accused to be given notice of allegations against him and an opportunity to be heard in answer to those allegations. The requirement can be excluded by clear and precise wording in the rules of the organisation, but if there is any doubt concerning the exclusion the doubt will be interpreted in favour of the complainant. In the absence of exclusion the notice of the allegation must be sufficiently explicit to enable the accused to understand the charge against him and to enable him to prepare his answer. He must also be given sufficient time before the hearing to get ready for it. The hearing itself need not be conducted in accordance with judicial rules of evidence, but the accused should be given opportunity to put his case and to challenge the case against him. A decision taken in contravention of the rule may be set aside.

One word of caution to an aggrieved party. The rules of natural justice are extremely complicated and it is by no means certain that they will be applied in every case. As already seen they can be excluded by the constitution of the organisation and the courts can also decide that they may be over-ridden if the complainant has not suffered any significant harm. They do, however, provide a judicial safeguard for any person who is likely to have his livelihood jeopardised by a decision of some organisation which controls the field in which he operates and, as Lord Denning has shown, in such a case the courts are conscious of their duty to be vigilant.

Chapter 9

BREEDING HORSES

To enter the business of breeding horses requires the services of a good accountant and lawyer almost as much as it requires sound practical knowledge and familiarity with pedigrees. It is essentially just as much a business as making nuts and bolts, but there are aspects of it which are unique and it is these aspects which will be examined in this chapter.

THE HORSE BREEDING ACT 1958

The Act, with its associated rules, applies to Scotland (except insofar as commons and the New Forest are specifically referred to in section 15) but does not apply to Northern Ireland. Its main provision is to require that every person who keeps a stallion, not being a thoroughbred or a pony of a prescribed breed, which has reached the age of two must have a licence or a permit for it granted by the Minister of Agriculture, Fisheries and Food. No licence or permit is required for a thoroughbred stallion, defined as one entered or eligible for entry in the *General Stud Book*, nor for a Shetland pony kept anywhere in Great Britain, nor for a Dartmoor,

Exmoor, Fell, New Forest or Welsh Mountain pony kept in an area specified in the First Schedule to the Horse Breeding Rules of 1948. Although generally no licence or permit is required for these exempt breeds in their prescribed areas, they may not be travelled for breeding purposes nor exhibited on any premises not in the keeper's occupation for breeding purposes without such a licence being obtained.

The Minister may refuse to grant a licence, or may revoke a licence, if it appears to him that the stallion:

(a) is permanently affected with any contagious or infectious disease; or
(b) is permanently affected with cataract, roaring, whistling, ring bone (high or low), side bone, bone spavin, navicular disease, shivering, stringhalt or defective genital organs, all being diseases or defects rendering the stallion unsuitable for use for breeding purposes; or
(c) has proved to be inadequately prolific; or
(d) is calculated, if used for breeding purposes, to injure the breed of horse by reason of its defective or inferior conformation or physique.

If a person is aggrieved by the refusal or revocation of a licence he is entitled to call for a referee's inspection. A member will then be chosen from a panel made up of veterinary surgeons and persons appointed after consultation with the breeding societies who will make a report for consideration by the Minister. After reading the report the Minister will either confirm or over-rule his original decision and this time his determination will be final.

Once a licence has been granted it is the Minister's duty to have the stallion examined at such intervals as he considers proper to ensure there are no grounds for revocation. In this connection there is one qualification to paragraph (b) above in that if the Minister is contemplating revoking a licence because a stallion is affected in its wind, he shall not do so if it has attained the age of nine and has been licensed for two years. The usual method of determining age is adopted, in that it is provided that the horse will be treated as having attained the age of one on the 1st of January next after the year in which it was foaled.

Instead of revoking the licence the Minister may impose a condition to the effect that the stallion shall not, for a specified period or until further notice, be used for breeding purposes. He will adopt this course when he is advised that the animal is temporarily affected by a disease or defect rendering it unsuitable for use, but that such disease or defect is likely to disappear. In this manner the Minister can safeguard the breed without putting the owner to the expense of a revocation followed by a re-application (section 4).

If the Minister refuses to grant a licence or revokes it for one of the above reasons, he may issue a permit as an alternative, if it appears to him expedient to keep the stallion entire. He has complete discretion as to whether to refuse or grant the permit and he can impose such conditions, including a time limit, as he thinks fit. If the keeper is unable to obtain either a licence or a permit he must have the stallion castrated once it has attained the age of two and, in default, the Minister may, after due notice, cause it to be castrated or slaughtered at the expense of the person on whom the notice was served (section 6).

Both a licence and a permit continue in force until:

(a) it is revoked by the Minister; or

(b) it ceases to be in force after a change of ownership (see below); or
(c) the stallion dies or is castrated; or
(d) the stallion has been outside Great Britain for a consecutive period of fourteen days or such longer consecutive period as the Minister may allow. For this purpose the consecutive period begins to run when it is put on board the ship or aircraft taking it out of Great Britain and ceases to run when it is landed on its return.

In addition to the above, a permit comes to an end when the period specified for its duration expires.

The reference to change of ownership in paragraph (b) is to the provisions of section 8 of the Act which enables the licence or permit to be transferred if the stallion is sold or let for a period of longer than six months. The section goes on to provide that if the transfer has not taken place within one month after change of ownership the licence or permit ceases to have effect. The transfer is made on application to the Minister and is effected by an endorsement on the original. On change of ownership the licence-holder or permit-holder must give notice to the Minister and he also has the duty to inform the Minister when the stallion dies or is castrated.

DISEASES OF THE HORSE

As the recent outbreak of contagious equine metritis shows, disease can have a crippling effect on the activities of the breeder. The law concerns itself in this field under two main heads, roughly divided between common law and statute. On the one hand common law seeks to apportion liability for the spread of disease, whilst, on the other, statute looks to the control and prevention of infection through the agency of the Diseases of Animals Act 1950 as amended in 1975.

In this respect the common law is seen to be pursuing its historic role in that it never operates in a vacuum and seldom to protect the welfare of the public as a whole, unless that end is achieved coincidentally by upholding individual rights. Before it will act there has to be injury suffered by one person arising out of the legally culpable actions or neglect of another, but given those circumstances legal sanctions will be applied in the form of damages.

In *Cooke* v. *Waring* (1863) it was established that the owner of an animal who knows the animal to be suffering from an infectious or contagious disease is liable in damages if he allows it to mingle with the animals of another. Prior knowledge is an essential of the offence, but if there is such knowledge damages will be awarded even where no attempt has been made to mislead or to cover up the condition – *Penton* v. *Murduck* (1870). The courts have decided from time to time that where knowledge of disease is present silence can constitute an offence, which is a departure from the more usual principle of *caveat emptor* requiring the injured party to rely completely on his own investigations. Because of such decisions it would be dangerous to send a horse known to be infected to a public market, or to stand an infected stallion, or to send an infected mare to a stallion, but in each case, as a prerequisite of a claim for damages, it is up to the plaintiff to prove that he has suffered loss from the defendant's actions.

Statute law is not concerned in the same way with the question of individual rights and liabilities. Through its two main instruments, the Diseases of Animals Act 1950 and the Diseases of Animals Act 1975, it aims to protect the public, rather than the individual, from the consequences of disease and it does this by giving the Minister of Agriculture, Fisheries and Food wide powers to prevent infection or, where this is impossible, to control and eradicate its spread. The 1950 Act is the principal one, with the 1975 Act extending and tightening its provisions to cover several loopholes which appeared over the years. The main purpose of the later Act is to extend the powers of inspecting premises where infected animals are believed to be and to define the Minister's role in making orders regulating the import of animals.

So far as horses are concerned the diseases covered by the Acts include glanders or farcy, equine infectious anaemia, equine encephalomyelitis, African horse sickness, dourine, parasitic mange, equine virus abortion and epizootic lymphangitis. Any person having in his possession or under his charge a horse affected by any of these diseases must report the fact with all practicable speed to the local police who must, in turn, pass the information on to the appropriate authority. It is an offence not to notify the disease, although it is open to the defendant to claim he had no knowledge of the infection and that he could not with reasonable diligence have obtained such knowledge. As knowledge is presumed it is up to the defendant to prove its absence and this might be difficult in a case where he had failed to call a vet to a horse suffering from unusual and persistent symptoms.

Following the notification an inspection is made by a veterinary inspector appointed by the Minister, whereupon the Minister has wide powers, through his inspector, to make suitable orders in an attempt to isolate the disease. The keeper of the horse must immediately separate it from non-affected animals and must treat any other horse which has come into contact with it in the manner prescribed by the Minister. The power to make orders is contained in section 10 of the 1950 Act which also enables the Minister to declare the stables in which the outbreak has occurred to be an infected place. Various orders made under the Act create legally enforceable rules to deal with the outbreak depending upon the sort of disease involved. Usually they provide for a ban on movement into and out of the infected place, for isolating the affected animal and its contacts, for erecting fly-proof screens and for making regulations concerning disposal of bedding, dung, fodder, clothing and anything else with which the animal may have come into contact.

In the case of glanders or farcy the veterinary inspector must cause the animal to be slaughtered unless the owner objects, in which case it must not be killed until the Minister gives further special authority. If it is killed compensation is payable to an amount depending upon whether the diagnosis was correct or not. If the animal proves to have been free from disease, full compensation is payable, but if it proves to have been infected only a proportion of its value can be claimed.

The breeder, hopefully, will very rarely be concerned with the foregoing provisions of the Diseases of Animals Acts, but the Acts are likely to affect him if his business becomes international. For obvious reasons, relating to the prevention of infection, the two Acts impose strict control on the import of animals, but, for reasons connected more with the prevention of cruelty, they also relate to export.

EXPORTING HORSES

Because the European Economic Community requires standardisation of regulations relating to the welfare of animals whilst in transit, Parliament has passed the Transit of Animals (General) Order 1973. Long before this, however, there were orders in force in this country made under the provisions of the 1950 Act providing for such welfare and these are still in co-existence with the 1973 Order. As an example the British Railways Board is under a duty to ensure that animals are properly supplied with water and food at such railway stations as the Minister may direct and it must also provide food and water at the request of the person in charge of the animals. That person must exercise his right to demand such provisions and if he allows his charges to go without water for twenty-four hours he is guilty of an offence. Similar regulations relating to food, water and ventilation are in force for sea and air transport with the general aim of ensuring that animals do not suffer unnecessarily on their journey. To this end it has been held in *M'Laren* v. *Smith* (1923) that it is the absolute duty of a ship's master to destroy injured animals, and in *British Airways Board* v. *Wiggins* (1977) that any person who has charge of the animal at any time during the journey, including the air company which flies it, has a responsibility to see that the container in which it is shipped is suitable for the purpose.

A person who exports horses has three separate considerations to bear in mind. He must ensure that the regulations concerning their welfare in transit as outlined above are observed, he must ensure that he knows of and complies with the requirements of the importing country and he must ensure that the exporting provisions of the Diseases of

Animals Act 1950 and of the Ponies Act 1969 are fulfilled. In connection with this latter requirement it is convenient to treat ponies and horses separately as there are some differences in the regulations relating to their export. Ponies are defined as horses of not more than 14½ hh.

To deal first with horses. Section 37 of the 1950 Act makes it an offence to ship or attempt to ship by sea or air any horse in a vessel or aircraft from any port or aerodrome in Great Britain to any port or aerodrome in Europe (other than the Republic of Ireland) outside the United Kingdom, the Channel Islands and the Isle of Man, without the horse first being examined by a Ministry-appointed veterinary inspector and certified by him to be capable of being conveyed to such port or aerodrome and disembarked or landed without cruelty, and to be capable of being worked without suffering. If the inspector finds the horse to be in such a physical condition that it is cruel to keep it alive, or to be permanently incapable of being worked without suffering, he may forthwith slaughter it.

Where the horse is found by the inspector to be a heavy draft horse, a vanner, a mule or jennet, or an ass it may not be exported unless he also finds it to be not more than eight years old and of not less than a certain value. At the time of writing the values are fixed by the Export of Horses and Ponies (Increase in Minimum Values) Order 1973 at £300 for a heavy draft horse, £200 for a vanner, mule or jennet and £120 for an ass. For ponies the minimum value is £160, or in the case of one not exceeding 12 hh (other than a Shetland pony not exceeding 10½ hh) £120, or in the case of a Shetland pony £60.

The above regulations relating to certificates and minimum

values do not relate to the following cases:

(a) exports to the Republic of Ireland or to a destination outside Europe – section 37(1) of the 1950 Act;
(b) the export of thoroughbred horses certified by the Jockey Club as having arrived in Great Britain not more than one month previously for the purpose of being run in a race; or being shipped for the purpose of being run in a race; or being shipped in order to be used for breeding purposes – section 40;
(c) the export of horses to be used as performing animals – section 37(4);
(d) the export of horses registered in a stud book of a society for the encouragement of horse breeding recognised by the Minister, and intended to be used for exhibition or breeding purposes – section 37(4);
(e) the export of a foal at foot accompanying a horse as in paragraph (d) – section 37(4);
(f) the export of horses which are being shipped to a port or aerodrome in the Republic of Ireland or outside Europe, or of horses which the Minister is satisfied are intended for exhibition, breeding, racing, jumping, riding or polo, or of a foal travelling with its dam if the dam is any such horse. The exceptions in this paragraph are contained in the Export of Horses (Excepted Cases) Order 1969, which to some extent duplicates the Diseases of Animals Act exceptions.

Where exemption is claimed on the grounds that the horse is to be used for exhibition, breeding, racing, jumping, riding or polo, the horse may only be exported if a permit is obtained and such permit is granted by the Minister on submission of satisfactory proof that the animal is in fact to be exported for that purpose.

The export of ponies is regulated jointly by the 1950 Act and the Ponies Act 1969. Their minimum value for export has already been considered and a pony cannot be shipped from any port or aerodrome in Great Britain to any port or aerodrome outside the United Kingdom, the Channel Islands and the Isle of Man unless the Minister is satisfied that it exceeds the minimum value and that it is intended for breeding, riding or exhibition and that immediately before its shipment it had been inspected and certified as capable of being carried to its destination and embarked or landed without unnecessary suffering.

In addition to the above the shipment of a pony registered in the stud book of the Arab Horse Society, the National Pony Society, the British Palomino Society, the British Spotted Horse and Pony Society or the breed society of English Connemara, Dales, Dartmoor, Exmoor, Fell, Highland, New Forest, Shetland or Welsh pony is unlawful unless there has been obtained from the secretary of such society a certificate that the pony is so registered.

IMPORTING HORSES

The Equine Animals (Importation) Order 1973, made under the authority of the Diseases of Animals Act 1950, makes it an offence to land or unload a horse in Great Britain from any country outside Great Britain, except under a licence issued by the Minister. The licence may be general or specific and may be made subject to conditions. The conditions imposed will generally be directed towards preventing the import of diseased horses or of horses which have run the risk of contact with diseased horses. In particular it is provided that the Minister may require a mallein test for glanders or farcy, except where the horse is being imported from Northern Ireland, the Republic of Ireland, the Channel Islands or the Isle of Man. A horse which is landed without a licence may be immediately re-exported on the directions of the Minister, or an order may be made providing for its detention and isolation.

Chapter 10

THE REGISTRATION OF FARRIERS

This final chapter must start with an apology for putting last in the book a subject which most horsemen would put first. The saying 'no foot, no horse' is one universally accepted, even by Parliament which passed the Farriers (Registration) Act in 1975 for the purposes set out in its preamble: 'To prevent and avoid suffering and cruelty to horses arising from the shoeing of horses by unskilled persons; to promote the proper shoeing of horses; to promote the training of farriers and shoeing smiths; to provide for the establishment of a Farriers Registration Council to register persons engaged in farriery and the shoeing of horses; to prohibit the shoeing of horses by unqualified persons; and for purposes connected therewith.'

To attain these objects the Act gives the general function of securing adequate standards and conduct amongst farriers to The Worshipful Company of Farriers, but it also establishes a Registration Council to compile and administer a register of persons engaged in shoeing, whether in the course of trade or privately. When the Act is brought into full effect entry in one or other of the four parts of the register will be an essential requirement for anyone who wishes to shoe horses as section 16 makes it an offence for a person who is not registered to carry out any farriery, and for a person who is registered in Part III of the register to carry out farriery by way of trade or for reward. Farriery is defined as any work in connection with the preparation or treatment of the foot of a horse for the immediate reception of a shoe thereon, the fitting by nailing or otherwise of a shoe to the foot or the finishing off of such work to the foot. The definition does not include trimming the foot if there is no intention of immediately fitting a shoe. The majority of the provisions of the Act are now in force but, at the time of writing, the all-important section 16 has not been brought into effect so an unregistered person may shoe horses for the time being but he will not be allowed to call himself a farrier or a shoeing smith – Farriers (Registration) (Amendment) Act 1977.

The Farriers Registration Council is created for the purpose of compiling and keeping the register up to date. For this purpose it can make rules relating both to the entry of names onto the register and the removal of names therefrom. It consists of sixteen members appointed from the bodies, employments and callings specified in Part I of the First Schedule to the Act, including, amongst others, representatives of The Worshipful Company of Farriers, persons engaged in farriery on their own account, persons employed in farriery, the Royal College of Veterinary Surgeons, the Jockey Club, the R.S.P.C.A. and the Council for Small Industries in Rural Areas. From its members the Council is required to appoint two committees, one for investigating disciplinary cases, and the other for considering and determining such cases. The Disciplinary Committee must consider any evidence brought before it by the Investigating Committee and it can, if the evidence supports the conclusion, direct that a name be struck from the register for any one of the following reasons:

(a) that the named person has been guilty of serious misconduct in any professional respect; or
(b) that such person was not qualified for registration at the time he was registered; or
(c) that such person has been convicted of an offence involving cruelty to animals.

Any person who is aggrieved by a direction of the Committee to remove a name from the register may appeal to the High Court in England or to the Court of Session in Scotland – the Act does not apply to Northern Ireland – and on the hearing of the appeal the court may make such order as it thinks fit, which will then be final and binding. A direction to remove a name from the register may specify a time within which no application may be made for re-registration, but even if it does not, no such re-registration can be effected without a specific direction given in that behalf by the Disciplinary Committee.

Procedure and evidence before the Committee must follow the rules laid down by the Council, and in formulating those rules Part II of Schedule 3 to the Act requires the Council to make sure they deal with the following points:

(a) to secure that notice that the proceedings are to be brought shall be given, at such time and in such manner as may be specified in the rules, to the person alleged to be liable to have his name erased from the register;

(b) to secure that any party to the proceedings shall, if he so requires, be entitled to be heard by the Disciplinary Committee;

(c) to enable any party to the proceedings to be represented by counsel or solicitor or (if the rules so provide and the party so elects) by a person of such other description as may be specified in the rules;

(d) to require in any case where it is alleged that a person registered under the Act has been guilty of serious misconduct in any professional respect and where the Disciplinary Committee judge that the allegation has not been proved, that they shall record a finding that the person is not guilty of such misconduct in respect of the matter to which the allegation relates;

(e) to ensure that persons likely to be affected by any finding of the Committee are duly notified of that finding.

QUALIFICATION FOR REGISTRATION

The main purpose of the 1975 Act is to create a register of farriers who, when section 16 is brought into operation, will be the only persons entitled to shoe horses. Those qualified to be included in the register are specified in the Act as amended by the Farriers (Registration) (Amendment) Act 1977 under four headings, as follows:

Part I of the Register

(a) those persons who on the 1st January 1976 were registered in the register of Farriers kept by The Worshipful Company of Farriers;

(b) those persons who satisfy such conditions as to apprenticeship or training or both as the Council may prescribe and have passed a prescribed examination;

(c) those persons who have completed a course of training as a farrier in Her Majesty's Army and have passed a prescribed examination;

(d) those persons who have been registered in Part II or Part IV of the register and have passed a prescribed examination;

(e) those persons who hold a qualification granted outside the United Kingdom and for the time being accepted by the Council and who have during any period of two years subsequent to the date when they obtained their qualification been regularly and gainfully engaged in the shoeing of horses.

Part II of the Register

A person may be registered in this part of the register if he applies for registration before such date as may be prescribed – (at the time of writing not yet fixed) – and satisfies the Council that during any period of two years before the date of his application or such shorter period as the Council may approve he was:

(a) otherwise than as an apprentice or while undergoing a course of training regularly engaged in the shoeing of horses in a business which consists exclusively of such shoeing or in the business of a blacksmith or general smith of which the shoeing of horses forms part; or

(b) practising as a farrier in Her Majesty's Army.

Part III of the Register

A person may be registered in this part of the register if he applies for registration before such date as may be prescribed – (at the time of writing not yet fixed) – and satisfies the Council by means of a certificate by a practising veterinary surgeon or by such other evidence as the Council may in his case consider appropriate, that during any period of two years before the date of his application he has regularly and competently:

(a) carried out the shoeing of horses belonging to himself; or
(b) otherwise than by way of trade or for reward carried out the shoeing of horses belonging to other persons.

Part IV of the Register

A person may be registered in this part of the register if:

(a) being a person who is not otherwise entitled to be registered under the Act he applies for registration before such date as may be prescribed – (at the time of writing not yet fixed) – and satisfies the Council that during any period of two years before the date of his application or such shorter period as the Council may approve he has been regularly and gainfully engaged in the shoeing of horses otherwise than as an apprentice or while undergoing a course of training; or
(b) being a person who has not passed a prescribed examination he applies for registration before the said prescribed date and satisfies the Council that he has complied with:
   (i) the conditions as to apprenticeship or training prescribed by the Council in accordance with paragraph (b) relating to Part I of the register; and
   (ii) such additional conditions, if any, as to further apprenticeship or training as the Council may require in his case.

To avoid hardship the Council has a discretion to waive the time limits fixed in relation to applications for inclusion in Parts II, III and IV of the register if good cause can be shown as to why those time limits were not observed. It should be noted, however, that no time limits have yet been fixed, leading to the inevitable query of whether farriers are registering in sufficient numbers to make the Act a viable proposition. To prevent unregistered persons from shoeing horses would lead to a crisis if there were not an adequate number of registered persons to undertake the job nationwide.

Appendix:

RIDING AND ROADSENSE

(Reproduced by kind permission of the Royal Society for the Prevention of Accidents.)

THE HIGHWAY CODE APPLIES TO ALL ROAD USERS

(The advice given here is supplementary to the Highway Code and is presented by The Royal Society for the Prevention of Accidents, in co-operation with the British Horse Society and the Pony Club, for the safety of horse and pony riders.)

RIDING ALONE OR IN A SMALL PARTY

Look ahead and ride straight.

Keep well in to the left.

Ride in single file if the road is at all narrow or has bends.

Leader walk or jog at a steady pace to avoid the rear file having to trot up fast.

Look both ways before moving off, turning or halting.

If trotting, go steady round all corners.

Have your reins short enough for your horse to be really under control.

Obey police, traffic control signals and traffic lights.

Give way to pedestrians at zebra crossings.

Look behind and in front before you pull out to pass a stationary vehicle, to make sure the road is clear.

It is *not* your road when a vehicle is stationary in front of you on your side of the road, i.e., a vehicle or person coming towards you has the right of way.

Ride on the grass verge where possible (some local councils forbid it).

In a built-up area be considerate for mown grass in front of houses and elsewhere.

If your horse shies, turn his head away from the object and *don't look at it yourself*.

You need not ride in silence *but* keep alert to road conditions.

RIDING IN A PARTY OF MORE THAN FOUR

Never ride more than two abreast.

Decide at once who will drop back to form single file when necessary.

Divide into columns of four or five.

Leave 100 yards at least between each column.

Put a steady horse in the lead.

Have beginners and/or small ponies in middle.

Leading and rear files make clear signals.

Leader set the pace. Keep it slow to avoid trotting or cantering up of the rear files.

Have nervous or traffic-shy horses on the inside.

LEADING

If leading another horse when mounted, have it on your near side and conform with other road users by riding on the left side of the road. When leading on foot, always place yourself between your horse and the traffic, and walk on the left-hand side of the road keeping your horse close to the edge.

Be careful when passing pedestrians, particularly so if your horse is difficult.

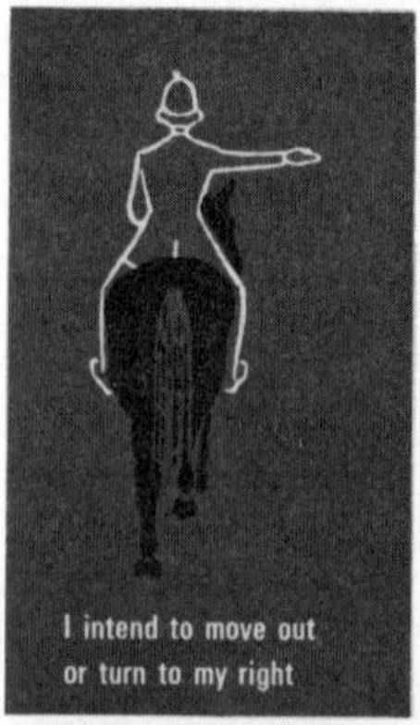

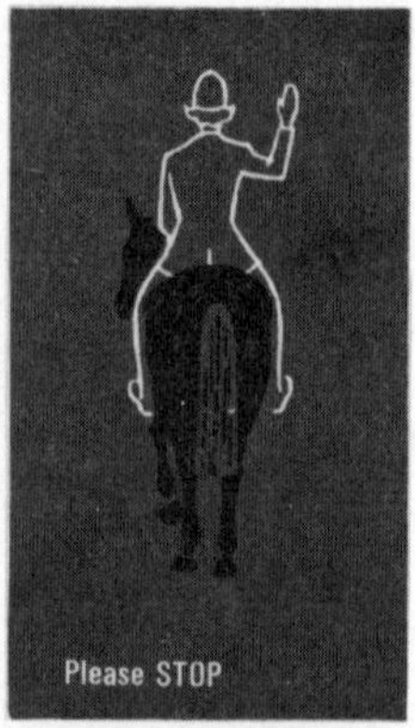

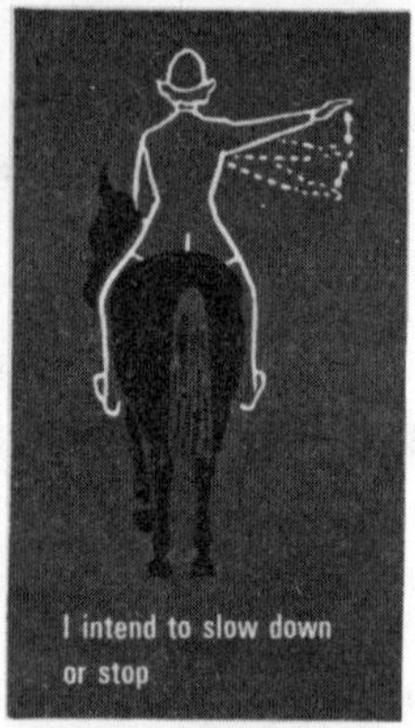

SIGNALS

These are the signals you should know and use. Give them clearly with your whole arm.

If, for the safety of all concerned, you think it is necessary for a motorist to stop, slow down or give you more room, you should endeavour to make this clear by signalling as shown in the drawing on the right.

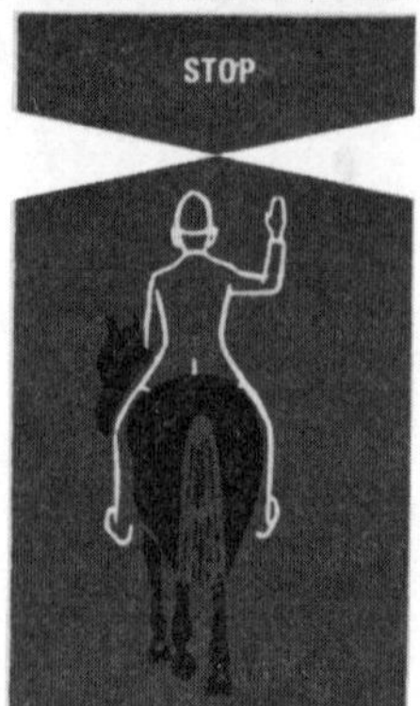

Pat your horse and speak to him if he is nervous of high vehicles.

Look ahead and walk straight.

CROSSING A MAIN ROAD OR AT A JUNCTION

At a main road or at road junctions, look right, then left, then right again before crossing or emerging. If the road is clear, walk quickly and straight across. If it is not, wait quietly, be alert and do not fidget.

If in a party, never start to cross a road until all the riders are near enough to cross together. Wait until the road is clear enough to allow the whole party to cross in safety.

Never get separated – some on one side of the road and some on the other.

RIDING OR LEADING AT NIGHT

Take special care on the road at night, in twilight or in fog and mist.

Carry a light which shows white in front and red to the rear. One specially made for attaching to the off-side stirrup is best.

Whether you have a light or not, tie something white, a handkerchief or rag, to your offside arm or stirrup. Better still, use a strip of reflective material and wear it as low as possible round the ankles or heels. A combined fluorescent-reflective band which can be worn on arm or leg is available from ROSPA.

The leader of a large party should carry a white light and the rearmost rider a red one.

RIDING OR LEADING ON A SLIPPERY ROAD

Get off it as soon as possible.

Trust your horse and let him walk on.

He does not want to fall. If you leave him alone he is less likely to slip.

On icy roads quit your stirrups.

If your horse falls, pick yourself up and let him get up. Pat him.

Do not try to mount where it is still slippery.

If leading, do not try to pull your horse along.

Hold the reigns lightly so that you can let go if your horse falls and walk on. He will follow.

Concentrate on keeping your own feet.

SNOW

Stop at a garage or farm. Ask for *thick* motor grease. Smear thickly on soles and frogs on all four feet. The snow will then not ball. If going far, do this more than once.

INSURANCE

It is advisable for every rider and horse owner to hold some form of third-party legal liability insurance. The rider might be considered liable if his horse or pony were to break loose or cause any damage to other people or their property.

BE COURTEOUS

Be considerate and help others on the road.

Acknowledge the courtesy of other road users with a gesture.

Pass others at a walk on a bridle path or narrow road.

HEADGEAR

In the interests of safety a hard hat should always be worn. Hats are now available bearing the British Standards 'Kite-Mark' label.

RIDING SAFELY

Take your British Horse Society Riding and Road Safety Certificate. Details from your County Road Safety Officer or British Horse Society County Chairman.

Three words to remember:

ALERTNESS – ANTICIPATION – COURTESY

INDEX OF STATUTES AND STATUTORY INSTRUMENTS

INDEX OF CASES

GENERAL INDEX